Alphonse M. Grussi

The Little Follower of Jesus

Alphonse M. Grussi

The Little Follower of Jesus

ISBN/EAN: 9783337300418

Printed in Europe, USA, Canada, Australia, Japan

Cover: Foto ©Lupo / pixelio.de

More available books at **www.hansebooks.com**

THE
Little Follower of Jesus.

BY

Rev. J. M. Grussi, C.PP.S.

THE VISITATION.

THE Little Follower of Jesus,

—BY—

REV. A. M. GRUSSI, C.PP.S.

A BOOK FOR THE YOUNG FOLKS.

BASED AND BUILT ON

"The Following of Christ."

—BY—

THOMAS A KEMPIS.

FIRST AND SECOND BOOK.

Cum Permissu Superiorum,

NEW YORK:
P. J. KENEDY,
Excelsior Catholic Publishing House,
5 BARCLAY STREET.

1889.

COPYRIGHT,

1889,

By P. J. KENEDY.

TO

His Eminence

James Cardinal Gibbons,

ARCHBISHOP OF BALTIMORE,

THIS WORK,

THE LITTLE FOLLOWER OF JESUS,

IS

MOST HUMBLY AND RESPECTFULLY

DEDICATED.

THE AUTHOR.

CONTENTS.

	PAGE
INTRODUCTORY	7
The Little Follower of Jesus	11

BOOK FIRST.—The Road Laid Out.

CHAPTER

I.	Despise the Vanity of the World	17
II.	Have a Humble Opinion of Yourself	21
III.	The Doctrine of Faith	26
IV.	Be Prudent in What You Do	31
V.	On Reading	36
VI.	Renounce Inordinate Affection	41
VII.	Avoid Vain Hope	46
VIII.	Friendship and Undue Intimacy	51
IX.	Obedience and Subjection	55
X.	Bridle your Tongue	60
XI.	Progress in Spiritual Life	65
XII.	Trials and Afflictions	70
XIII.	Resisting Temptations	76
XIV.	Rash Judgment	81
XV.	Works Done out of Charity	86
XVI.	Bearing the Faults of Others	92
XVII.	Vocation	98
XVIII.	Example of the Saints	104

XIX.	Exercises of a Good Christian	108
XX.	Silence and Solitude	112
XXI.	Sorrow of Heart	117
XXII.	Human Misery	122
XXIII.	Thoughts on Death	127
XXIV.	Judgment and What Comes After	132
XXV.	Amend Your Life	137

BOOK SECOND.—Steps Towards Jesus.

CHAPTER

I.	Interior Life	145
II.	Humble Submission	149
III.	A Peaceful Disposition	153
IV.	A Pure Mind and Simple Intention	158
V.	Self-Consideration	163
VI.	Joy of a Good Conscience	167
VII.	Love of Jesus Above All Things	172
VIII.	Familiar Friendship with Jesus	177
IX.	Want of All Consolation	182
X.	Gratitude for the Grace of God	188
XI.	Lovers of the Cross	193
XII.	The Royal Way of the Cross	199

The Flowers	207
Angels' Dialogue on New Year's Night	214
The Legend of St. Christophorus	233

INTRODUCTORY.

MOST of what I would like to say, by way of introduction, is already contained in that first article under the title of the book—"The Little Follower of Jesus." Here I would add only these few remarks.

First: These articles were begun about a year and a half ago, and were printed, piece by piece, in the *Little Crusader*, the same children's paper that my other stories, entitled *Drops of Honey*, first appeared in. As you will notice, the work is not yet complete. You have here only the First and Second Books. It will take me at least two years more to finish the other two books, the Third and Fourth. God willing, they will be got ready for you by-and-by. In the meanwhile, make good use of this part of the work.

Secondly: The whole of the work, by the time it is completed, will make a rather large and thick book; hence, I made the publisher the following proposal: To divide the whole work into two parts, the First and Second Books of it to be given out in one volume, the Third and Fourth, later on, in another. He agreed and was very well satisfied ; and therefore you have now the First Volume of the *Little Follower of Jesus.* It is sent out ahead, to prepare the way, so to speak, for the Second Volume, which will follow in about two years, or as much sooner as it can be got ready.

Thirdly : One particular feature of this work, which is not mentioned in the first introductory article, and that I wish, therefore, to call your attention to here, is this : I try, in every chapter, to introduce a little story— one that has a bearing on the subject treated in that chapter. These stories, I trust, will more fully awaken the interest of the readers, and keep their minds fixed more and better on the instructions and admonitions that are given. Most of these stories are taken from an excellent German work, called, *Mehler's Beispiele.*

Fourthly : This work, *The Little Follower of Jesus,* is intended to be a book of spiritual reading, particularly for the young folks. How should you use it, therefore? Try to read at least one chapter every day. Before you begin to read, kneel down first and say a short prayer to the Holy Ghost. Think that God is present, and that He is about to speak to you from the book. Then read the chapter slowly and attentively. When you have finished reading, close the book, and spend a few minutes in thinking over what you have read. Do this, and the book, with God's grace and blessing, will be of great benefit to your souls.

May Jesus bless us all!

The Little Follower of Jesus.

FOR some time past, I have been reading a certain little book which, I suppose, many of you know, or at least, of which you have heard—the golden book, as it is called, of *The Following of Christ*, by Thomas à Kempis.

This book, so full of God's holy spirit and truth, has been, and is still, a guide for thousands of pious souls on the way to sanctity and perfection. But for children who have not yet received the full gift of understanding, and who, therefore, are not able to study over and meditate on the truths contained in this book, I rather think it is too high: they cannot yet reach its sense so as to draw the precious fruit out of it.

Yet, a person, you know, ought not to wait till he is grown up to become a follower of Christ. No; the earlier he begins with it, the better. Jesus, our Saviour, is the Model for us all to imitate; and, indeed, if this divine

Model were placed before the children quite early, as soon as their minds develop, and they begin to understand—placed before them in a lively manner, so that they will take interest in it, and would thus be led to study the life of their Redeemer, don't you think a great deal of good would be done in the world by such a work? I am sure, it would soon help to increase the number of true, devout Christians, followers of Christ.

Let us suppose, here is a young man who is given to bad ways. He has acquired wicked habits, which have already brought death to his soul, and which, maybe, cause him to be a scandal to others, a disgrace to our holy religion, and to his name of Catholic. What now? Speak to him of the following of Christ, tell him to set before himself for imitation the beautiful life of our blessed Redeemer: what good will it do? He will not even listen to you; and you might as well preach the *following of Christ* to a stone or a tree—it would do just as much good. But, had he been trained to it when he was a child; had you then set before him for imitation the lovely model of our Saviour's life; had you then often instructed him, and called his attention to the beauty of virtue as represented in the model; had you then kindly taken him by the hand, and pointing to Jesus going ahead, led him forward on the way; had you done all this then, when the young man was yet an innocent child, don't you think he might be a good Christian now, leading a pious, holy life, saving his own soul, and, perhaps, the souls of many others?

Oh, yes! It is very important that the children, God's little ones, should learn and be led to follow the foot-steps of Jesus Christ. Therefore, while reading the *Following of Christ*, as I have said, it occurred to me that, maybe, with God's blessing, I could do something for the little ones, to benefit their souls in this way. I have studied the matter over for a long time; now I will tell you what I will do, and how:

I will take the *Following of Christ*, and read a chapter out of it; then I will close the book and meditate for a time on what I have read; then I will sit down to write a chapter for you, my dear little reader of the *Crusader*. I will try to get a chapter ready for you every week; and it will always, as near as I can make it, treat on the same matter as the corresponding chapter in the *Following of Christ*. The title of each chapter shall remain the same, excepting where I might think it proper to change a word—without altering the sense, however—so that you may more easily understand it. And I will also try to bring in from the *Following of Christ* whatever is suitable, and as well as I can arrange it. For the rest, I will speak to you and instruct you in my own style; and I will endeavor, if possible, to close each article with a verse or a few lines from that chapter on which I had been writing. Now, this is my plan.

And, because I intend to place before you, in as lively and interesting a manner as I can, Jesus, our blessed Saviour, for your imitation, and, at the same time, to lead you on and teach you how to follow Him, I will call the whole work "The Little Follower of Jesus." Do you understand it all now?

I trust with God's help, if He lets me live and keeps me well, that I can carry the work through and finish it. May he bless my feeble efforts, and let all be to His honor and glory!

Book First.

THE ROAD LAID OUT.

I.

Despise the Vanity of the World.

MY child, there are two roads before you. On the one you see Jesus, your Redeemer, who loves you so much. He goes ahead of you, and beckons you to follow Him. On the other is the world, which also loves, or rather pretends to love you. It, too, is winking, and coaxing you to follow it. "He that followeth Me walketh not in darkness," says Jesus. "Come, follow me," the world says; "let us enjoy the good things present." To whom will you listen? Which will you follow?

A child was once looking at the rainbow. See! the end of it comes down way over yonder, in that field, where the walnut tree stands. People told her that if she would go where the end of such a rainbow was, she would find something beautiful—a costly treasure. So, now, she would just run over to the walnut tree, and see what she would find in the end of the rainbow. She hurries over; and when she reaches the tree, she is tired and nearly out of breath; and she looks around for the treasure.

But the rainbow is gone; and there is no treasure, nor anything beautiful as she expected. She is awfully disappointed.

Do you know what vanity is? Vanity means something empty. If there is anything you think is worth something, or you think there is something of great worth in it, and you find out it is not worth anything at all, or there is nothing at all of worth in it, why, then, that is what we call a vanity.

Now, Jesus invites you to follow Him; the world coaxes you to follow it. Jesus says, He will teach you, and give you many good things. But these good things are yet hidden. First, He wants you to follow Him; then He will let you taste these good things by-and-by. Jesus, and His Spirit, and His teachings, and the good things He possesses, are all hidden manna. You will find out how sweet this manna is only when you have tasted it.

But you must not turn away from it. Because you often hear about this manna, and you never see anything but what looks poor and insignificant, you might think there is nothing in it, and you might go by and let it alone, and not care anything about it.

First of all, Jesus wants you to be humble.

Even if you knew the whole Bible by heart, and could tell all the smart things that the great men of the world have said, your Saviour would not want you to be the least bit proud about it. He says Himself: "I resist the proud; but to the humble I give My grace." Therefore, first of all, if you want to be a follower of Jesus, and taste of the hidden manna, you must be humble.

But the world also makes you promises. It says: "Look here, little one! my goods are not hidden. They are open before you: you can see them, taste them, possess them. I will give you riches and honors, and any pleasure and amusement you can desire. I will give you a long life of happiness, real, lasting happiness. Follow me, and I can assure you, you can always sing: "I am as happy as a big sun-flower!"

Beware, my child! Do not listen to this voice. What the world promises you is nothing but vanity. It has fooled many a one, and brought him into misery; and he was sorry for it only when it was too late. Listen to Jesus, and follow Him on the road He leads you. With Him you will find your true and only happiness

"Vanity of vanities," says Thomas à Kempis, "and all is vanity, but to love God and Him alone."

II.

Have a Humble Opinion of Yourself.

SOME saint, I believe it was St. Philip Neri, heard a certain Sister praised very highly for her virtues. People said she was a real saint; and the fame of her holiness was spreading all around. St. Philip wanted to find out how much truth there was in the reported sanctity of this person; he wanted to try her virtue. What did he do?

He put on old, patched clothes, an old crumpled hat, and a pair of torn boots—sure, he looked like a real beggar, and nobody would have the least idea that this was St. Philip—and in that guise he started off to visit the Sister whose holiness he heard people praise so much. Before he came to the convent, he took care to wade through a mud puddle, to dirty his boots, and thus to give them a worse appearance than they already had.

When the portress opened the door and asked what he wanted, he told her he wished to see that Sister about whose virtues and sanctity people were talking so much, that he had something particular to say, about which he wanted her counsel. Accordingly, the nun was called.

"Poor man! what can I do for you?" she asked.

"Would you, please, just pull off my boots?" St. Philip asked in return.

"What, you beggar! I pull off your boots? Get out of here as fast as you can!" and she left the "beggar" and went out of the room, not a little angry.

"Aha! well!" thought the Saint to himself, "the sanctity of this Sister is not so very deep. The foundation is wanting. She is not humble."

Do you see now, my child? I told you the last time that, if you want to be a true follower of Jesus, first of all, be humble. But to be or to become humble is not so easy. The virtue of humility can be more easily talked about than acquired. Yet it is true, and you can see it from what I have told you about St. Philip and the nun, that without humility you cannot become holy, you cannot become a true follower of Jesus.

Now, then, what will you begin with? You want to become humble, for you want to be a follower of Jesus. First, you must always have a humble opinion of yourself. And how can you get it? Jesus will help you to it; just ask Him for grace. But you must also think over the matter yourself. Study and try to find out how much you are worth. If you find out that, as to your body, you are worth nothing, it will not be hard for you to get a humble opinion of yourself.

I said, as to your body; for if we regard your soul, you have an infinite worth. And what are you as to your body?

Remember, I pray you, first, that whatever gift you think you have, you received from God. Your body itself comes from God; He created it for you, body and soul. If you think you have lovely eyes, a fair complexion, fine hair, and so on, do not forget that they come from God. You gave nothing to yourself: God gave it all to you. He might have created you without these fair gifts, and he can take them from you at any moment, if he wants to. And after all, what will the fair gifts of the body that you possess be reduced to in the end? To worms and ashes! Think of it. Therefore, the fair complexion you would some times be proud of is only a covering for worms and ashes.

And what about your mental gifts? Maybe

you have good talent; you can easily beat others in learning. And you will learn many things, till you are grown up. Perhaps you will be, some day, what we call a philosopher: you will know wonderful things about the stars, and the animals, and the plants, and many other things; and people will praise you for your knowledge. But ask yourself: Who gave me the talent to learn? Was it not God? I did not give it to myself. And God can take it from me at any moment. What reason have I, therefore, to be proud?

You cannot do even the least good work without God's grace helping you. All that you can do—ah! yes, and haven't we all done it so many, many times?—without His aid, is to offend him by committing sin. Is that something to be proud of? Then, it should not be hard for you to have a humble opinion of yourself.

And never think yourself better than another. That boy or girl may have fewer bodily gifts than you have, but just for that very reason he or she may be more pleasing to God than you are. Never despise one that you know is a sinner. He may be converted and become a saint; and you may become worse than he is and be lost. "To think nothing of ourselves," *The Following of Christ* says, "and always to judge well and highly of others, is great wisdom and high perfection."

III.

The Doctrine of Truth.

I SUPPOSE you are going to school, and you are learning to read and to write.

In course of time, if you persevere, you will learn many more good and useful things. Maybe you are even now studying arithmetic and geography, grammar and book-keeping, natural philosophy, and some such useful branches. This is all very good; and certainly it is God's will that you should learn such things. He has given you a good talent to learn, and He wants you to use it.

But you have never read what Thomas à Kempis says. Here are the words: "Knowledge is not to be blamed, nor simple acquaintance with things, which is all good in itself and ordained by God; but a good conscience and a virtuous life are always to be preferred."

Do you see? All the learning you may have or get, and let it be ever so big a heap, unless it helps you to lead a good life, will do you no good. The more you have learned, the greater will be the account you must give to God one day. So, then, go ahead and learn all you can, and ask God to help you and to keep you from learning what would not be good for you. You may need all you can learn now some future time, when you have entered the position or state of life that God has called you to. But—here comes a but—you must not forget. You must also learn to become humble, obedient, kind, patient, pure, and holy; you must learn to pray and to love God and your neighbor; in short, you must learn to become a true follower of Jesus. Yes, and this is just the principal thing you must learn. If you have not learned this—to become a true follower of Jesus—all the rest that you have learned can help you nothing.

Now, who will teach you? Do you think you can learn this science—the science of the saints it is called—from books? Certainly, there are books which give you instructions how to become a follower of Jesus. But you must have a teacher: and your Teacher is Jesus Himself.

Jesus is the eternal Truth. He says: "I am the Way, the Truth, and the Life." He will speak to you and instruct you; He will teach you how to become a true follower of

His—how to become a saint. Just you listen to Him, and do what He tells you.

Sometimes He speaks through your father and mother, through your teacher and through the priest. When they tell you something that you should do or not do, it is just as much as if Jesus Himself tells you: "He that hears you, hears Me;" and He also said: "He that despises you, despises Me."

Sometimes Jesus speaks to you Himself. You cannot hear His voice with the ears of your body; but you can hear it in your heart. He will open your mind and give you clear thoughts; and He will touch your heart and move you to do His will. You will learn to know Jesus better, His goodness, His infinite love for you, and what is His holy will. And you may learn it this way better than if you should study the best of books.

Especially, the more humble you are, the more Jesus will love you, and the more He will reveal Himself to you and teach you. You know what the Blessed Virgin sang? "He hath regarded the humility of His handmaid; for, behold, from henceforth, all generations shall call me blessed."

Yes, even though you could not read a single

word, could not even spell, you could learn more of Jesus and how to be His devoted follower, than the smartest, most learned man in the world. Have a humble heart, and have a desire, a burning desire, to learn God's truth : Jesus Himself, the eternal Truth, will teach you.

Did you ever hear the story about St. Bonaventure and Brother Giles? This Brother had no learning at all; but he was very humble, child-like, and good-hearted. One day he said to St. Bonaventure:

"My reverend Father, you are very happy ; you learned theologians can love God much more than we can, and work out your salvation much more easily."

"You are mistaken, Brother Giles ; for, with the assistance of grace, every one can love God as much as he will!"

"What!" exclaimed the good monk, "poor ignorant creatures, who can neither read nor write, can love God as perfectly as those who have made studies?"

"Why, certainly they can ; and, moreover, a poor peasant may sometimes love God more than a learned theologian."

At these words good Brother Giles feels

himself transported with joy, and runs to the garden, opens the door that leads to the street, and begins to cry out as loud as he can:

Halloo! poor people, halloo! good women who can neither read nor write, come and hear the good news: If you choose, you can love the good God as much as any theologian, and even as much as our reverend Father Bonaventure!"

Here, for the conclusion, is a passage from *The Following of Christ:*

"The more a man is united within himself, and interiorly simple, so much the more and deeper things doth he understand without labor; for he receiveth the light of understanding from on high."

IV.

Be Prudent in What You Do.

A TEAM of horses, that had been tied to a hitching-post before a tavern, broke loose and ran away. The wagon was broken, the harness torn, and the horses themselves were hurt. Why did they run away? and why did they cause such a damage? A man came riding along on a bicycle; and that scared them. But that little scaring they got would not have caused any further damage, if the driver had been on the wagon to take care of his horses and to manage them. Where was the driver? He had stepped into the tavern to cool himself off, and to get a lunch. So you see, the whole mishap, and the damage caused by it, came because the driver was not on the wagon to guide the horses.

Now, my child, to be a true follower of Jesus, it is necessary that you should be prudent. Do you know what prudence is? As often as you want to say or do something, and before you do it, you consider well what would be the best way of saying or doing it, that is, the way it would be the most pleasing to God, and most beneficial to yourself and to your neighbor; then you will try to say or do it that way, so as to remain in peace with yourself and with your neighbor. That is about what is meant by being prudent.

Prudence is a great virtue. It is a moral virtue, and that is, it adorns our souls and gives beauty to our lives. It is one of the cardinal virtues. Cardinal comes from the Latin word "cardo," which means hinge. Just as the door rests on the hinges and turns on them, just so, also, must our lives and the virtues we strive to practise rest and, so to say, turn on the cardinal virtues, one of which is prudence.

You must, therefore, be prudent in all that you say, and in all that you do. Without prudence you cannot exercise any other virtue as it ought to be; you cannot lead a holy life, such as God wants you to lead. St. Bernard calls prudence "the driver of the other virtues." Just as I told you above about those horses: they ran away, broke the wagon, tore the harness, and hurt themselves, because the driver was not there to guide them; so you will be apt to run into fatal mistakes with all the virtues you may have or may be trying to practise—you may bring yourself, your precious soul to ruin—if you have not the virtue of prudence to guide you.

Yes, indeed, my child, it is very important that you should have this virtue of prudence. What must you do to acquire it?

First, you must pray earnestly for it. It is, partly at least, a gift that Jesus can give you. But He gives this gift, as He gives all others, only to those who are humble. He says: "I confess to Thee, Father, Lord of heaven and earth, because Thou hast hid these things from the wise and prudent, and hast revealed them to little ones."

Secondly, you must have a true love for God and for your neighbor; and for this, certainly, you must pray always and earnestly. The more you love God, the more pains you will take to consider, before you say or do anything, what would be most pleasing to Him. And the more truly you love your neighbor, the more you will try to say or do things so that they will do him most good, and avoid what could offend him. And if, nevertheless, by anything you have said or done, your neighbor should be offended, even against your will and when you cannot help it, the humility that is in your heart will help you to bear his reproaches and hard words patiently, and by kindness to gain him and to restore the peace that has been broken between you. Truly, a heart that is humble and loves God is a prudent heart and enjoys constant peace and happiness.

Well, what would you do if you had this virtue of prudence? You would not so easily believe the bad that is spoken to you about others. You would think: "There is nobody that has so many faults as I have myself." And therefore you would rather close your eyes against the faults of others, and only try to see the good that is in them. Much less would you play the tell-tale, that is, carry to others what you have heard or seen, and you think is bad. That is imprudence, first-class—and sin.

Another thing: You would not want to know everything best yourself, and think there is nobody ahead of you, and smarter than you are. You would, on the contrary, distrust yourself; you would ask the advice of others, and be guided by it.

Here are a few words from *The Following of Christ*, well worth remembering: "The more humble one is in heart, and the more in subjection to God, so much the more prudent will he be in all things, and the more at peace."

V.
On Reading.

NOW, I know you are only yet a little child, maybe just beginning to go to school; or, supposing even you have been going to school already for several years, yet you are hardly old enough to be allowed to read the Holy Scriptures. When you are older, and you can better understand, then nobody will forbid you to read the Bible. You will even be admonished to do so—to read the Catholic Bible, and to study it, and to draw all the fruit from it that you can for your soul.

I suppose your parents have a Bible at home? Maybe it is a fine, large book, and has many beautiful pictures in it; and your parents allow you sometimes to take the book, and go through it, and look at the pictures. Well, remember, the Bible is the holy word of God. It tells you about Jesus, and how you are to become His disciple and follower. It is, therefore, a most holy book; and you must take care to handle it with the greatest and deepest respect. St. Charles Borromeo, I believe, it was, this great saint in the Catholic Church, that always, in humility and out of respect, opened and read the Holy Scriptures kneeling. But, in the meantime, study your Bible history well, and thus prepare yourself to read the Bible when you are older.

But there are other good books, and papers also, easier than the Bible, that you may and should read, even now, while you are yet a child. You do not need to wait till you are grown up and have a better understanding. It is even very important that you should acquire a relish and love for good reading while you are young, living in the days of your childhood. Why?

You want to become a follower of Jesus while you are yet young; you do not want to wait till you are old, do you? You have been told already that it is Jesus Himself who will teach you how to become His follower. One way that he teaches you, is: He speaks to you through good books and papers. But you cannot hear Him speak if you do not read those books and papers, or somebody else does not read them to you.

There are many good books printed, and quite a number of excellent, little story papers given out, any of which would be very good and just suitable for you. I trust, your parents have already bought several such books for you, and they are getting at least one such paper. If they have not, why, then you must ask them to do so. Sure, if you tell them you want to become a follower of Jesus, they will buy you some good books, and get you a good little paper. But what use to make of your books and paper? That is the next question.

Here are a few rules: First, always have a good intention when you read. You should read for God's honor, and for the welfare of your soul, and not read merely out of curiosity and to while away the time. Secondly, you must have more regard for what you are reading, that is, for the truth of what is said, than for the person who wrote it, or the way in which it is said. Do as *The Following of Christ* directs: "Inquire not who may have said a thing, but consider what is said." Thirdly, do not let the reading hinder you in doing something else that is your duty. "Katie," a mother said to her daughter, "take out this feed to the chickens." "Oh, ma, wait a minute, till I have finished reading this story," said the little girl. Do you see? That was wrong. This girl should have put her book or paper away immediately, and done what her mother wanted her to do. Obedience goes above everything else.

Fourthly, do not be too greedy. A boy was reading a story-book, and he staid up late, and kept on reading and reading, and his parents could hardly get him to go to bed. And then he neglected to get his lessons for school, and he did not say his night prayers half well enough, and he even dreamed about what he had read. You know well enough, such reading is wrong.

Lastly, never read what is bad. Do not try to smuggle books or papers into the house, and read them privately, when you know it is a sin for you to read them, and your parents would burn them if they knew you had them, and they could get hold of them; and they would punish you, besides. "Tell me," says St. Chrysostom, " what sort of company a person goes into, and I will tell you what sort of a person he is, because he is sure to be like the company he keeps." Books and papers are company, too, are they not?

"If thou wilt derive profit,"—words from

Thomas à Kempis,—"read with humility, with simplicity, and with faith, and never wish to have the name of learning."

VI.

Renounce Inordinate Affections.

HEAR what Jesus, our Master, says: "If any man will come after Me, let him deny himself, and take up his cross, and follow Me." And again, "Take up my yoke upon you, and learn of Me, because I am meek and humble of heart; and you shall find rest to your souls." Yes, my dear child, little follower of Jesus, this is a lesson for you—and, indeed, for us all. If we wish to follow our Saviour, we must deny ourselves, renounce our passions, inordinate desires, and affections. But what does this mean?

A boy was once riding a young horse. The horse was proud and wild, and not yet fully broken. You know how such an animal will act when there is somebody on his back riding him. So this horse, too, would throw up his head, and then bend it stubbornly; he would take a start as if to run; and then, again, he would stop, and go a few steps back, and turn crossways on the road.

But the boy was not afraid: he had courage. He sat firm in the saddle; the horse could not throw him off. With a steady hand he held the bridle reins; the horse could not break through and run away with him. Young, and big, and stout as the horse was, he felt that the boy was his master, and he had to let himself be governed. So you see, by his firm will, and steady determination, and undaunted courage, this boy mastered and even tamed the young, wild horse, that was, maybe, four times as large, and more than four times as strong as he was.

Now you can more easily understand, I suppose. There are different kinds of affections, and desires, and passions in our hearts; and they are called inordinate when they are opposed to reason—common sense—and to the law of God. They are, therefore, bad; and if we are not on our guard, they will mislead us, and bring us into sin. To preserve ourselves from ruin, we must let God's grace and our own reason and conscience hold the reins tightly on us: we must govern ourselves, check our evil inclinations, overcome our passions, and thus avoid sin. That is what is meant by "renouncing our inordinate affections, denying ourselves, and following Christ."

What do you think? Quite a difficult task,

isn't it? A continual warfare; a lifelong struggle. Ah, yes; but this life battle against ourselves is a most glorious thing, and, if persevered in faithfully to the end, will bring us a great reward. You cannot be a follower of Jesus unless you undertake this life struggle against yourself. Open the "Lives of the Saints," and point out to me, if you can, one saint who did not fight this battle—denying himself, renouncing his inordinate affections, taking up his cross and following Jesus.

Well, then, what must you do? First, you must learn to know yourself. You cannot renounce your inordinate affections and evil passions if you do not know them. Therefore, you ought to examine yourself every day; and because, maybe, you could not, after all your examining, find out your evil inclinations, passions, and bad habits yourself, it would be well to get your parents, or those who take your parents' place, to help you. Ask them, and they will tell you; for they know—or, at least, ought to know—what bad traits you have.

Let us suppose you have a hasty temper. You get angry at every little thing; and then you say harsh words, and you quarrel and call names; and, maybe, you will even strike your brother, or sister, or playmate, and push them away from you. Do you see? This is one little enemy already that you must fight with and subdue—your evil temper.

Or you have too fine and too great an appetite for eating and drinking. You frequently take too much. More than once you got sick from eating half-ripe fruit and berries. You always ask for dainties; and what does not suit your taste, you let stand and will not touch. You also got into the habit of taking things on the sly—sugar, cakes, jelly, and so on. "Johnny," a mother once asked her little son, "did you take the piece out of this pie?" "No, ma'am." "Then, how did this hole get into the pie?" "Oh!" said Johnny, drawing his sleeve across his face, "I s'pose it got 'wore' in." So this inordinate appetite is another enemy you must overcome; and I know he will give you enough to do.

I might go on and count up for you a great many more of such enemies, as pride, self-will, deceit, envy, laziness, and so on.

Undoubtedly, pride and anger are our greatest enemies, and the hardest to subdue. Therefore, Jesus says: "Learn of Me, because I am meek and humble."

Set to work earnestly, now. Find out what are the evil inclinations and passions in your heart, and then say with a firm will: "Out with them! Jesus, help me!"

"It is by resisting the passions," says Thomas à Kempis, "and not by serving them, that true peace of the heart is to be found."

VII.
Avoid Vain Hope.

A LITTLE boy, once, just for fun, wanted to build himself a play house. His father had bought several hundred bricks to erect a chimney, and they were piled up out in the yard. The boy set the bricks one against the other; and then another row on top of the first, and so on, until he thought his house was about high enough. He also divided it off into several rooms, by putting bricks in between, for partitions. For the roof, he set up the bricks on ends, and made them lean over from both sides, until they came together, and rested against each other at the top. With that he had his house finished. What happened? Fox comes running up—Fox is the name of their dog—and he brushes against the house and knocks it down. Just imagine how angry the little boy got. "You old, nasty dog!" he exclaimed. "You must just come along and knock down my house. Go away and let me alone!"

You are yet only a child, a little boy or girl; but, perhaps, you parents are already making great plans about you. They intend you to become this or that; and they will educate you so, and give you such a schooling, that you may once make a fair show in the world.

You are too young yet to make any, or very many, plans yourself. You leave everthing to your parents, and to those who are older than you. It is something very beautiful, very touching, to see how simple and artless children are. They know nothing about themselves; and they can do almost nothing, they are so little; and therefore they trust their parents, and those who are older and grown up, in everything; they believe what they hear them say, and try to imitate what they see them do. Such a little child is like the ivy that clings to the thick, stout oak-tree.

But when you get older, you will begin to make plans for yourself. You will make yourself a great name in the world. You will try to become rich; you will strive to become a great statesman, or a poet, or a philosopher, or gain renown in some other of the many ways. To make your way thus in the world, you will rely greatly on your own genius and ability. You will also ask advice of other smart men; and you will use those who are not so smart as you are as instruments to help you forward. All these things may come, or, at least, you may be tempted that way many a time, and, if you do not take care, easily misled. This is the way of the world; it pretends to be your friend, but it is a treacherous enemy. It gets you to build a house; and you think it is fine work, and you have made a success of it; and just when you think you have finished it, and you are safe, and now you can enjoy yourself at ease in your fine house, the world will shake it, let it fall down over your head, and all your vain and empty plans will go to nothing. Think of the boy I told you of, building his brick play-house.

What I want you not to forget is this: There is some one else who has better and quite different plans for you, and who intends to make something great and glorious of you. It is He whom you have undertaken to follow—Jesus, your Saviour. What He wants to make of you, you cannot yet tell; neither can I, nor anybody else. Just give yourself over entirely and willingly to Jesus, and let Him guide you; He will lead you right; and you will be great on earth and in heaven.

In Paris there was a certain young man, called Francis Xavier. He also had great plans, how he would become a wonder of learning, and make himself a great name in the world. There was another young man, some years older than Francis Xavier, called Ignatius, and he had the spirit of Jesus, and had just entered on the right way to holiness. One day Ignatius whispered into the ear of Francis Xavier these words:

"What doth it profit a man if he gain the whole world, but lose his precious soul?"

And day after day, as often as he met him, he repeated to him these same words, until Francis began to think them over himself, and they worked in his soul, by the grace of God. They brought about a great change. The young man left the way of the world, and turned his back on it, to follow Jesus. Our Saviour had his plans for him, too; and you know what the young man became: a great saint in the Catholic Church—St. Francis Xavier, apostle of India.

Do you see now, and understand? Jesus has His plans and intentions for you, too, most certainly! What must you do, on your side, that they may be carried out?

First, give up all vain hopes. Make your resolution even now never to strive after honor and glory in the world, or to gain for yourself a great name. Learning is good, and riches may be good, and honors, but only as far as Jesus wants to let you have them. You must not seek them for the world's sake.

Secondly, do not put too much trust in yourself. Do not rely on your own knowledge and ability. Do not despise others, nor think yourself better than everybody else. Be humble! give yourself into the hands of Jesus, and let Him do with you according to His holy will. "The foolish things of the world hath God chosen, that He may confound the wise; and the weak things of the world hath God chosen, that He may confound the strong," St. Paul says.

Here is a word for you from *The Following of Christ:* "It will do thee no harm to put thyself below everybody, but it will hurt thee very much to put thyself before any one."

VIII.

Friendship and Undue Intimacy.

HE that feareth God shall likewise have good friendships: because, according to him shall his friend be." How true are these words of holy Scripture, and how worthy of our consideration!

My child, if you look about you in the world, and observe only a little the ways and doings of men, you will see much that one might think is friendship. Experience, however, teaches that of this so-called friendship only a small part is real and true. The greater portion is nothing more than a fine outside dress, often put on to hide the baseness of a false inside.

Two men happen to meet, some day, on the street. They are so glad to see each other; they shake hands; they talk so friendly, and are so polite; they laugh and make fun, and talk about their families, their business, and what not. When they leave, they shake hands again, and "hope to see each other again soon; and you must not forget to visit me sometimes," and so on. You know, and you can see every day for yourself, how such business is carried on.

Now, what do you think? These two men are the best, most intimate friends, are they not? It would seem so. But you are mistaken: they are not. Hardly have they parted, when one says: "Why in the world did I just have to meet him?" and the other says: "Well, if he isn't a bore! I shall not forget to visit him sometimes." Do you see? Of such friendship there is plenty in the world.

Yet, to have a true friend is to possess a great treasure. "A faithful friend," says the Wise Man, "is a strong defense; and he that hath found him, hath found a treasure." My little follower of Jesus, it is not wrong for you to have such a friend, or more than one— many, if you can find them. On the contrary, it will be very good for you. A true friend will ever be a great help for you in the work of your life—the following of Jesus. What must you do to find one?

First, begin with yourself. Let it always be your first and main endeavor to have God for your friend. Always have Him before your eyes; ever walk carefully in His presence. Never let yourself be led into mortal sin: that would be losing or casting from you your greatest blessing, God's love and friendship. Fear your Creator all the days of your life. "The fear of the Lord is the beginning of wisdom," says the Psalmist.

Also, you must not forget to cultivate a most intimate friendship with your holy guardian angel, with your patron saint, with your Mother, the Blessed Virgin, and with those other saints for whom you have a special regard. Often think of them. Pray to them every day.

Secondly, guard yourself against the false friendship of the world. Avoid the company of bad men. "Evil communications corrupt good manners," says St. Paul. You cannot have Jesus for your friend if you wish to be a friend of the world.

If you fear God, and try to keep yourself from sin, it will not be hard for you to find good friends. They will find you, or you will find them, without seeking one another. It is with these friends as it is in general. "Like loves like," according to the proverb.

It is not good to be altogether intimate with even your good friends on earth. You should be closely intimate with God and your other heavenly friends. But with men on earth it is not good to be too friendly. "Be in peace with many," says the Holy Ghost, "but let one of a thousand be thy counsellor." It is best to reveal the secrets of your soul only to one human being on earth—the priest, your spiritual father and confessor.

Here is a passage from *The Following of Christ* for every little follower of Jesus to consider : "Sometimes we think to please others with our company ; and we begin rather to be displeasnig to them from the bad qualities they discover in us."

IX.

Obedience and Subjection.

I HAVE now come to a chapter, my dear reader, which, for us, is of as great importance as any of the others that we have so far gone through in *The Following of Christ*. Do you know the virtue which so pleases our Saviour, and which He teaches us so beautifully and expressly by His own example? It is the virtue of obedience. Jesus " humbled Himself, becoming obedient unto death, even the death of the Cross."

I will not say anything now about the obedience and subjection one must practise in religious life, that is, living as a Brother or Sister consecrated to God in a monastery or convent. You are yet too young to know what God may call you to in the future. But so much you ought to know and remember even now: Wherever you are, whether you are young or old, whatever station of life you may embrace to serve God in, you will be subject to authority, more or less, as long as you live, and always have the chance and the duty to practise this beautiful virtue of obedience.

Begin right away, in earnest. First, there are your parents, your older brothers and sisters. Be prompt in your obedience? Whenever father or mother calls you, let everything else be dropped immediately, and go. Do not let them call you twice. If they tell you to do a thing—now, I am suppossing that what they tell you to do is always right—do it right off, and do it well, not in too great a hurry and only half. If they tell you to stay away from a certain place, or to avoid the company of a certain person, then obey them punctually. Let no one prevail on you to go in the least against the commands or even the wishes of your parents, however much he or she may pretend to be your good friend. Next to God, you have no better or greater benefactors on earth than your parents. You must first listen to them and obey them, before you listen to and obey anybody else.

A boy once, coaxed by a companion, took a ride on the cars, against the expressed will of his mother. She was very much grieved. She corrected him for his fault, and then she punished his as he deserved. The boy always remembered that—not so much how his mother had punished him, as that he had grieved her by his disobedience. He often thought of it in his after-life, and he was sorry for it as often.

You should also obey your older brothers and sisters. Suppose you should try to represent to yourself, as often as your brother or sister asks you to do anything, that it is Jesus Himself who is asking you. Wouldn't you find it easier to do it?

Your obedience must be willing. Many children obey only after putting on long, sour faces, and after much pouting; and even while they are doing what they have been told to do, or leaving off what they are told not to do, they are dissatisfied inwardly, they complain to themselves and grumble. "Many are under obedience," says Thomas à Kempis, "more out of necessity than charity, and such have suffering, and are apt to murmur." Do you see? Such obedience is worth nothing in the eyes of God. Therefore, put away all sour faces, and pouting lips; instead, put on smiles and pleasantness, for Jesus' sake.

I will not say anything about obedience and subjection in school, and toward spiritual superiors. A child needs only to practise obedience faithfully at home, and I am confident, obedience in school, and wherever else it may be required, will come of itself.

Also, you must not stick to your own notions or opinions so tightly. Some children are thus. They will hold fast to their own opinion, and not give in to anybody. Such children, generally, cause a good deal of disturbance and trouble at home by their stubbornness and self-will. Give your opinion; say what you think you have a right to say, and then be done with it. To dispute long with others for every little thing is unpleasant for them as well as for yourself, and ill becomes a little follower of Jesus.

There are many people who cannot find peace nor rest. They always have trouble with somebody. They think, if they could go somewhere else, perhaps out into the wilderness, where they would be alone by themselves, and nobody to disturb them—then they would live in peace. A great mistake! It is not places or persons that will give you peace : your own heart must give it to you. Exchange your self-will for the humility and obedience of Jesus, and you will have peace and quiet in your heart everywhere and at all times. Do not forget this, my child. "If God is amongst us," says the *Following of Christ*, "we must needs sometimes give up our own opinion for the blessing of peace."

X.
Bridle your Tongue.

EXPERIENCE teaches us that great results, both in good and evil, oftentimes come from small beginnings.

Some years ago one of the largest cities in our country was almost entirely destroyed by fire. How, do you think, did the fire get started? A woman, they say, was out in the stable late in the evening, milking her cow. For some reason or other, the cow got contrary and began to kick; and it happened that she struck the lantern that the woman had set behind her on the floor. From the lantern the straw caught fire; and pretty soon the whole stable stood in flames. It was too late to quench the fire; it passed from house to house, until nearly the whole city was one sea of fire. Do you see? From the little flame in the lantern came the big fire that nearly destroyed a great, large city.

St. James says: "The tongue is indeed a little member, but it boasteth great things. Behold, how small a fire kindleth a great wood!" And the wise Man says: "A wicked word changeth the heart: out of which four manner of things arise: good and evil, life and death; and the tongue is continually the ruler of them."

Is there anything smaller, more insignificant, we might think, than a word? What harm can there be in a word, one little word? Ah, yes, great harm, unspeakable harm, may be in it!

Suppose you have spoken in anger only one harsh word; thereby you have offended one of your friends, companions. The mutual friendship between you is dead; a cold, hard feeling takes the place of the former love in your hearts; you no longer speak to each other, or even look at each other; and, where may it end? in hatred and enmity.

Or you have told an untruth, maybe it was a word of tale bearing; thereby you have disunited friends, sown discord among families and neighbors; it may end in deeds of blood and revenge.

Or it was a wicked, impure word, and thereby you have scandalized one of God's little ones. The poor child, innocent heretofore, learns the sin from you; he tells others; and so the sin goes on farther, and God only knows where and when it will stop! You are the one that started the sin; you gave the scandal first; and to you must be applied the words of our Saviour: "Woe to him that giveth scandal!"

My little follower of Jesus, after considering all this, do you not think it is a duty for us to bridle our tongues? What does this mean, to bridle our tongues? It means: We must govern them, check them, and not let them always say just what they please, without thinking before whether what they want to say is good or bad, whether it may do harm or not.

You must not say: "I am too young, too little!" I know that you cannot carry out exactly the advice that *The Following of Jesus* gives us, "Fly as much as possible the tumult of men. If thou hast leave to speak, and it is expedient, speak those things that may edify." You cannot lock yourself up at home for hours, to keep silence. You must go to school, and you must be in company often, with your brothers and sisters, and with other children; you must run about, and play, and enjoy yourself. I know all that. But, nevertheless, young and little as you may be, you must learn to bridle your tongue. What should you do, therefore? Here is a good rule; you can easily learn it by heart, and with a little earnest will and effort you can practise it:

> If you would lead a life discreet,
> Five things observe with care:
> Of whom you speak, to whom you speak,
> And what, and when, and where.

Suppose you wanted to correct some one, a boy or a girl, for some fault, or, as it may be your duty to do, you want to tell your superior about it; then consider well beforehand what you will say, and how you will say it. There are times when it is forbidden to speak; there are places in which to speak unnecessarily would be irreverent. Let it be your rule: I will never speak in school during school hours, nor in church, unless I am asked something, and I ought to speak. Is this rule hard to keep? Not if you want to keep it.

And sometimes, when you long to go out into company, to pass your time in idle talking, you might, on purpose, stay at home and in silence, and by good thoughts converse with Jesus.

"If any man offend not in word, the same is a perfect man," say St. James.

And Thomas à Kempis asks: "Why are we so so fond of speaking and talking idly together, when we yet seldom return to silence without some wound to conscience? I would that many a time I had kept silence, and had not been in company."

XI.
Progress in Spiritual Life.

"GLORY be to God in the highest; and on earth peace to men of good will!" thus the angels sang at our Saviour's birth. Isaias, the prophet, says: "A Child is born to us; and His name is called the Prince of peace." And at the last Supper Jesus said to His disciples: "Peace I leave with you, My peace I give to you: not as the world giveth, do I give to you." What does all this mean?

It means that, by His death on the Cross, Jesus freed us from sin, and procured for us peace and true happiness. He offers peace to His followers; and we can all get it and possess it, if we wish!

As we heard once before, peace and quiet of heart do not depend on just certain persons and certain places. Some persons think: "Oh, if I could live at such and such a place, away from such and such persons, then I'd have no trouble, then I could live in peace." A heart that strives to keep itself freed from sin, that loves God, and is subject in all things to the will of divine Providence, has peace and rest at all times and in all places. Sin alone takes away or prevents peace and happiness.

In a monastery there once lived a monk who also could find no peace. He was always in trouble with somebody. One day the thought came to him: "If I were somewhere where I could live alone by myself, and there was nobody to disturb and bother me, then I could be quiet and live happily. I will go out into the desert and live in the solitude as a hermit."

Consequently, he left the monastery, and went out several miles into the desert. He found a lonely cave near a fountain of water; and there he took up his abode. He stored away the provisions he had brought along, and arranged his cell to suit the life of a hermit.

It all went well for a time. One morning he went out to the fountain to fill his jug with water. Near the fountain there grew a sort of fine, delicious berry; and some of these he wanted to gather to take home with the water. He set the jug down on the ground, but it would not stand: it fell over. Again he set it up, and again it fell over. Already his temper was rising. He set the jug up a third time, and a third time it fell over. He snatched up the jug, and hurled it against a rock, smashing it into a thousand pieces.

However, he soon recollected himself. He began to think over what he had done.

"Do you see now?" said he to himself. "You cannot find peace and satisfaction even alone by yourself here in the desert. And why not? I understand now. Peace must come from myself. As long as I am ruled by sinful passions, I shall find peace nowhere. I must, therefore, overcome my evil inclinations, my passions; then I shall be happy. I will return to the monastery, to begin a new life. Under my superior and amongst my fellow monks, I can have more and better chances to struggle with my passions, and will obtain greater and stronger help from God to overcome them."

He went back that same day; and the story closes by saying that the monk, after that, enjoyed more peace and happiness in one year than he had enjoyed in all the years together that he had lived in the monastery before he made that trial in the desert.

What does this anecdote teach us? If we want to have peace and happiness of heart, as much as it can be obtained on this earth, we must fight against sin, overcome our evil passions.

Therefore, my little follower of Jesus, let us begin. First of all, let us not look too much at others ; or, as *The Following of Christ* has it, let us not " busy ourselves with the sayings and doings of others, and with things that concern us not." We have enough to do with ourselves. At least, if we do sometimes notice faults in others, and try, out of charity, to correct them, let us not forget that we have plenty faults ourselves, greater ones than we think and are inclined to believe. Let us not " look for the mote in our brother's eye, while we forget the beam in our own."

I told you before, in the chapter about " renouncing inordinate affections," what you should do to find out your faults, bad habits, passions, and evil inclinations ; you might read that over once more, just now. So, then, begin, and do not give up. " If every year we rooted out one fault," says Thomas à Kempis, " we should soon become perfect men."

And, here is a secret I will reveal to you. You ask : " What is the surest and best way of doing much good for the spiritual welfare of others ? " The surest and best way is : Begin with yourself! Just as you yourself make progress in spiritual life, so will you also work at the spiritual progress of others.

God arranges it so: He lets you work good for others while you are working good for yourself. You think you are doing nothing, because all your time is taken up with yourself; but imperceptibly, by God's grace, you are doing much good for others, for those that are living with you, round about you.

For the conclusion let us have another word from *The Following of Christ:* "The Lord is ready to help them that fight, trusting in His grace; who Himself provideth us occasion to fight, in order that we may overcome."

XII.

Trials and Afflictions.

HERE, now, is something that you have heard more than once: We cannot go through this world without having to bear, each of us, his share of trials and crosses. One may live only a few years, or he may live many years—all the same: every one has to suffer.

Trials and afflictions come in many different ways. One is subject to trial from sickness and ill health: there is hardly a day in the year that he can say he is quite well, and that he must not suffer from some one bodily ailment or other. There is another whose bodily health, maybe, is good enough; but, that awful scourge of poverty! He has not wherewith sufficiently to clothe, nourish, or shelter himself; he suffers great want. Others, again, are continually persecuted by their fellow-men. Whatever they undertake, they never succeed with it. Everything turns against them. In spite of their best efforts to get ahead in the world, they cannot; they rather go backward.

If only this were all! Many a man, besides

the load of outward or temporal afflictions that he has to carry, must bear a heavier cross of inward spiritual troubles. There are strong passions to conquer; great temptations to overcome; his own weakness to support; dangerous occasions to avoid. And this inward struggle of the soul frequently lasts for years. Many a one would gladly sacrifice all his worldly possessions if he could thereby rid himself of this spiritual cross. He strives honestly to serve God, to live as a good, pious Christian ought to; and yet—this heavy burden to carry!

Where do these trials and afflictions come from? They may be caused by one's own sins. You may be the maker of your own cross by the sins you commit. Or, God may send you these troubles to punish you for the sins you committed formerly: He gives you a chance to atone for them. Or, maybe, God lays these crosses on you merely to try you; thereby He wants to give you chances to gain greater merits for heaven. The devil does not like to see one lead a good, pious life, either; and, therefore, he also comes to trouble you. He puts all kinds of stumbling-blocks in your way, that you may fall and hurt yourself. God permits him to do so; but he can go no further than God allows him.

Here are a few passages from Holy Writ on this point: "Man, born of woman, living for a short time, is filled with many miseries," says Job. And St. Paul says: "Whom the Lord loveth, He chastiseth; and He scourgeth every son whom He receiveth." And again: "All who live piously in Jesus Christ shall suffer persecution."

What do you think now, dear children? Do you expect, if you want to be true followers of Jesus, that you shall have nothing to suffer in this world? Our Lord Himself said: "Ought not Christ to have suffered these things, and so to enter into His glory?" And "the servant is not greater than his lord. If they have persecuted Me, they will also persecute you."

Therefore, you may get ready. Trials and afflictions will come upon you. When they come, bear them patiently. If you get sick, and your pains are great, be as quiet as possible, and resigned to God's holy will. Do not complain, much less murmur. Do not trouble your folks too much, those who have to wait on you, by being peevish, and making them every little thing. Take your medicine willingly, even though it may be bitter. In such and all other trials be patient and resigned. Remember that one " My Jesus, Thy will be done!" said piously in time of sickness or other afflictions, is more pleasing to your Saviour, and more meritorious for yourself, than ten " Our Fathers " and " Hail Marys " might be at a time when you have nothing to suffer.

Do not measure your cross with that of others. Everybody has his cross to bear, you may be sure of that; but you should not become dissatisfied with yours, and wish you had some one else's cross to carry, because you think it is so much lighter than your own. The cross that God has put upon you, or permitted to be laid upon you, is just the right one for you; it suits you better than any other would.

There was once a man who also was dissatisfied with the cross that God had sent him. He always thought, and often said, that he had the heaviest cross to carry; others hadn't half as much to suffer, and they weren't any better than himself; and he couldn't see why he alone should have to suffer so much. Thus he complained and murmured against God.

One night he had a dream. He was in the

midst of a large field. On that field was an almost countless number of crosses fastened in the ground. An angel—it was his own guardian angel—appeared to him, and said: "You are ever complaining about the cross that God has placed upon you. You say it is too heavy. The crosses that others have are much lighter than yours. Now you shall have your choice. Come with me, and try the crosses in this field. You can pick out for yourself the one that suits you best."

The man did as the angel told him. He tried one cross after another. One was too heavy, another was too sharp at the edges, another was too rough, etc. At last he found one that was just right, just as he himself wanted it to be; it was neither too heavy, nor was it too pointed, nor too rough. It was just the cross that suited him.

"Take it, then, and carry it patiently," said the angel. "Do not complain any more; for it is just the very cross that God has put upon you, and that you have so often complained about."

"It is good for us," says *The Following of Christ*, "to have some troubles and adversities now and then; for oftentimes they make a man enter into himself, that he may know that he is an exile, and place not his hopes in anything of the world."

XIII.
Resisting Temptation.

"FIRE trieth iron, and temptation a just man." These words of Thomas à Kempis are nearly the same as those of the Wise Man: "The furnace trieth the potter's vessels, and the trial of affliction just men."

A saintly hermit, a devout servant of God, was once led by his guardian angel into a large city, there to visit a certain monastery. The monks of this monastery were renowned for their piety and holiness. What was the hermit's astonishment! He saw the whole place just swarming with little moors—more devils than you would see flies swarming about a cup of honey, or bees about a hive. There were devils in the chapel, devils in the choir, devils in the refectory, devils in the dormitories, in short, devils all over.

They left the monastery; the angel led the hermit through the other parts of the city. Still greater was his surprise! In the whole large city he could not see another single demon—not until they came to the gate where they wanted to go out. There the hermit found one devil, leaning comfortably against the wall, apparently taking it very easy.

"It seems you have good times," said the hermit to the devil.

"Yes, as good as I can wish them," answered the latter.

"How happens it that you take it so easy? In this city there are thousands of people living; and yet you are the only one devil here, and you seem to have nothing to do; whereas in the monastery there is comparatively but a small number of monks, yet there are so many devils, hundreds of them, and all seem to be very busy, to have much to do. How is this?"

"That is easily explained," replied the devil. "In the city I have engaged a large number of wicked men to help me. They do the work for me. The people, in general, do not resist temptations: they are easily misled. But in the monastery it is not so. There we have nobody to help us; and all the monks strive to be virtuous—one helps the other in this. They resist our temptations; and that takes so many devils, and gives us so much work.

My little follower of Jesus, isn't this something remarkable, something that we ought to consider well? God is good, and He means well with us when He sends us bodily or temporal afflictions. I said enough on this point in the last chapter. We ought to thank Him, the good God, every time He bestows such a favor on us. But when He permits such inward trials, temptations of the spirit, it is a still better sign that He loves us dearly, and, as our best and kindest Father, is concerned about our eternal welfare.

What does God intend when He permits temptations? Thereby He wants to help us root out the evil that is in us, rid us of bad habits, subdue the sinful passions and evil inclinations of our hearts; He wants to purify our intentions, perfect our virtues. He wants to give us chances to gain greater merits for heaven.

He permits the devil, therefore, to tempt us. The devil could do very little himself, if he had not some one to help him. He has two powerful helpers, and he engages them—the world and our own corrupt nature. But, I must repeat again, the devil, in tempting us, cannot go further than God permits him to go. God never allows him to tempt us above that which we are able, as St. Paul says; and He is always at our side with His grace, ready to help us overcome the temptation.

Just those who try hard to be good, to lead virtuous lives, have to suffer most from these attacks of the devil; and, you understand, it is quite natural. The devil, so to speak, runs a great risk every time he tempts one. He thinks, perhaps he can bring you into sin; and then you will lose all. If you resist and overcome his temptation, why, then, in spite of himself, he has helped you to gain new merit for heaven. You may imagine how the devil froths and rages when, instead of leading you to sin by his temptation, he has helped you thereby to something good and meritorious. There is nothing he dislikes more than this: helping people to get to heaven.

What should you do, then, when the devil tempts you? Resist bravely! You must not fear him. Say only once, "Jesus, Mary, and Joseph, protect me!" that will make the tempter flee immediately. You must be prompt, very careful. You dare not be half and half, wanting to play with the temptation and yet not sin.

Especially, you must try to accustom yourself to resist the temptation at the very beginning, not wait until it gets stronger, and will be hard-

er for you to overcome. A certain poet says:
> "Resist beginnings: all too late the cure,
> When ills have gathered strength from long delay."

"Little by little," says *The Following of Christ*, "doth the malignant foe gain full entrance, when he is not resisted in the beginning."

You must not be down-hearted, and lose courage when you are tempted. The greater the temptation, the more reason you have to be satisfied, nay, even to rejoice. God looks upon you as being strong in spirit; and He wants you to become stronger still. Look about you, and examine. Can you find one saint who was not severely tried, either by bodily affliction, or spiritual trouble, or by both together. I will conclude with the following admonition, given us by Thomas à Kempis: "Let us, then, humble our souls under the hand of God in every temptation and tribulation; for the humble in spirit He will save and exalt."

XIV.
Rash Judgment.

THE children were having Catechism instruction.

"What is the matter?" the priest asked a boy who was holding up his hand.

"Mary Watson is looking in her book."

"Close your Catechism, Mary, and put it away at once," said the priest. "But how could you know she was looking in her Catechism, Fred? She is sitting just behind you."

"I saw her looking," said the boy.

"You told on her, and by that you tell on yourself," continued the priest. "You could not have seen her looking in the Catechism unless you looked around yourself. That proves that you have not paid attention as you ought to have done. She looks in her book, and you look around: what is the difference? Both of you do wrong by not being attentive."

My dear children, we are all too ready to look about and watch others and find out their faults; and in so doing we forget ourselves, our own faults and imperfections. *The Following of Christ* repeatedly calls attention to this point, and lays great stress on it: That we should not busy ourselves so much with the faults of others, but rather and much more and more closely look after ourselves.

"Turn thine eyes back upon thyself"— words from the first book, fourteenth chapter— "and see thou, judge not the doings of others." You know very well the rule Jesus has given us: "Cast out first the beam out of thy own eye, and then shalt thou see to cast out the mote out of thy brother's eye."

We cannot help it, certainly: we sometimes hear others saying something, or doing something, that appears to us or that we know to be wrong. It is, then, nothing out of the way to judge of the thing itself; what is wrong is wrong, as far as the thing or matter is concerned, be it word or act. But we do not stop there, we go further. We pass over the word or action, and judge the intention, and that is wrong, that is rash judgment.

A person may have said or done something that was wrong in itself, outwardly; but we cannot look into the inside, we cannot see the intention. Maybe the person does not know that such a thing is wrong; maybe, behind this ignorance, if I may say so, there lies hidden the very best of intentions. Therefore, we must be careful. We may judge a thing to be wrong, and, if a favorable occasion presents itself, and we think our effort will be of avail, we may instruct the person and show how and why it is wrong; but we have no right to judge the intention.

Another thing to be considered is this: we all have our own notions, feelings, and likings. To these notions, feelings, and likings we are apt to hold fast. Our self-love makes us cling to them; to give them up is the hardest thing for us to do. We try to persuade ourselves that everybody else ought to think, feel, and like as we do. This inclines us to judge rashly of others. We even go so far as to misinterpret the good deeds of our neighbors; we close our eyes to the good deed itself, saying that there is a wrong intention underlying it. How very sinful this is! How unworthy of one who professes to be a follower of Jesus, who says: "Judge not, and you shall not be judged."

From these rash judgments frequently arise great difficulties and disturbances. Friends are separated, families disunited, and discord is sown among neighbors. My little follower of Jesus, beware of rash judgment.

What should you do to avoid such sin and trouble? First, never make it your business to observe others—never, unless God has made it one of your duties to do so. Parents must have a watchful eye on their children, teachers on their pupils, and all superiors on their inferiors and subjects; it is their duty, and therefore their business.

If something bad is done, and it is not known who did it, do not make it your business to ferret out the perpetrators, unless it is your duty to do so. Such detective business frequently leads to grievous sin. You know what it is to sin by false suspicion.

Secondly, if you happen to see or hear something that is wrong, then, if you can, and there is any prospect that it will do good, speak to the one that has done the wrong, and correct him in brotherly charity. If the evil is great, and it threatens to do great injury to the soul of him who does it, then it may be your duty to tell your superiors about it—the parents, the teacher, or the priest, according to circumstances. But, do not forget that you must never misjudge another's intention.

Thirdly, strive to purify your own heart. This I put last, this time; it ought to come first. In all that you do, try to have a pure intention—the honor of God, the welfare of your neighbor, and your own spiritual good. Thomas à Kempis says: "Many secretly seek themselves in what they do, and are not aware of it." You ought to make yourselves aware of what you are seeking.

Do not give up until you know all your faults, evil habits, bad passions, inclinations to evil. Judge yourself, but not others. And Jesus, our merciful Redeemer, will give you the grace to persevere in this war with yourself, and help you to gain the victory!

"In judging others a man toileth in vain; for the most part he is mistaken, and he easily sinneth; but judging and scrutinizing himself, he always laboreth with profit." These are words taken from *The Following of Christ*; are they not true?

XV.
Works done out of Charity.

OUR blessed Redeemer, we sometimes might think, gives us quite contradictory rules to follow and practise. For instance, He says: "Let your light so shine before men, that they may see your good works, and glorify your Father who is in heaven." Then, again, He says: "When thou givest alms, let not thy left hand know what thy right hand doeth." Does not this seem to be contradictory? We shall do our good works so that our fellow-men may see them, and yet we should also hide our good works, so that, as it were, even our left hand might not know what the right hand is doing. The following little story may help you to understand our Saviour's meaning with regard to the above two passages:

The editor of a daily paper one day received the following note, sent to him privately through the mail:

DEAR EDITOR.—Will you please forward the enclosed sum of ten dollars to that poor woman whose husband, lately, was run over by the cars and killed? The widow being thus, herself and children, left without a supporter, is in sore distress and suffers great want; this donation will, I trust, go some way in relieving her and her poor orphans. I ask nothing in return but their blessing and prayers. From

A Friend.

The widow's grateful answer, as published in the paper next day, was this:

Dear Editor.—The widow and her orphans wish hereby publicly to express their most heartfelt thanks for the charitable gift of ten dollars sent us. The money was duly received and it was more than enough to satisfy our present wants. Though our benefactor is unknown to us, and will not reveal himself, God knows him, and has noted his work of charity. All we can do is, as our benefactor himself requests, to bless him for his charity and to pray for him. This we will do as long as we live. May the good God reward him, even here on this earth, a hundredfold!

See, my little followers of Jesus, this is an example from which you can learn how you may give alms, or do good some other way to your fellow-men, so that your left hand will not know what your right hand is doing. How beautiful is such charity! How happy it must make him feel who practises it! How pleasing it is to God, and how richly He will reward it!

In that same city there lived a man who was very rich. God had blessed him with an abundance of wealth; and, thanks be to the same good God, he knew what use to make of his wealth. The man was as charitable as he was rich.

Did people know he was charitable? Yes. How did they find it out? There was never a good work of charity to be done in the congregation, or in the city, but this rich man took part in it. On the list of contributors, his name generally stood at the head. He was always liberal; his contributions, on comparing, were always found to be the largest.

As often, however, as he contributed to public charity, there was always one thing he principally aimed at: he never wished people to find out how much he had given. They might know that he had contributed, but they should not know how much. Sometimes, in spite of his efforts to hide it, it would come out anyway, and then, when people would admire him for it, and praise his charity, he was very much displeased, and seemed to be pained about it.

But still greater was this man's private charity to the poor, the sick, the afflicted of any and every class. He was, therefore, venerated by all, and loved as a father. His greatest pleasure was to help the poor in such a way that no one might find out whence the charity came. God only should know it; that was enough for him. Well, can you guess now from whom those ten dollars came, that were sent to the widow and her children, by the editor of the daily paper? They were the gift of this rich man. Here, then, my dear children, you have an example both of how you should let your light shine among men, and also how your right hand can do good without your left hand finding it out. Do you understand now what Jesus means?

Oh, if there were only more of such charity in the world! Poor people would not complain so much and so often of hard times, poor wages, poverty, and distress. My dear readers, make a firm resolution to practise this charity as often as you can, and as long as you live.

This is what you ought to remember: First, you must strive always to live in the state of grace. If you had had the misfortune to commit a mortal sin, then make an act of perfect contrition right away, and go to confession as soon as you can. Not mentioning that as long as you are in mortal sin you are in danger of eternal damnation, you can gain no merits for heaven by any good that you do in that state of sin.

Secondly, do the good work with the best intention, from the purest motive. Your intention should be: "All out of love to Jesus, to honor and glorify God!" Do not seek the praise of men; hide your good works from them as much as you can. People may know that you have given, for the sake of the good example; but do not let them know, if you can help it, how much or what you have given.

Thirdly, give in the right disposition. Do not ask: "How much are others giving? I will give as much as he gives." No. Give what you can, be it much or be it little, and give it with a good will. Do not measure yourself with others. First you may view your own circumstances and ability, and then turn your eyes wholly to God. Do not say: "If I were better off, if the times were not so hard, I would give more." Give what you want to give, or can give—simply, willingly, gladly!

For the conclusion, reflect on these words from Thomas à Kempis: "Without charity, the outward work profiteth nothing; but whatever is done out of charity, be it ever so little and contemptible, it is all made fruitful, inasmuch as God regardeth more out of how much love a man doth a work, than how much he doth. He doth much who loveth much."

XVI.
Bearing the Faults of Others.

"IF thou canst not make thyself what thou wouldst be, how canst thou expect to have another so exactly to thy mind?" asks *The Following of Christ*. This question, my dear readers, hits the nail right on the head, as we say. Don't you think so, too? We are all so much that way; we want everybody to have patience with us, to bear with our annoying ways and manners, but we ourselves will have patience with nobody; everybody and everything must be so smooth, as not to give us the least offence. But that is not the spirit of Jesus.

Open the gospels and read the life of your Saviour, study it carefully; you will find that, among the many virtues He exercised, this one of patience in bearing with the weaknesses and faults of others shines forth as one of the brightest. What patient forbearance, for instance, did He not exercise towards His apostles!

He had them about Himself, nearly day and night, for three years. He takes the greatest pains to instruct them, to explain His doctrines, to lay before them plainly his mission, that He has come to suffer and die for the redemption of mankind. He endeavors to draw them away from earthly pursuits, to fill them with his own spirit, to make them understand the mission on which they themselves are to be sent, to convert the world for Him, to lay down their lives for His holy religion. How dull is their understanding! How wrong many of their notions! How awkward their doings, and how childish, sometimes, their talk!

At one time, during a storm on the lake, they wake Him up, saying: "Lord, save us, we perish." Jesus calls them: "Ye of little faith!" Peter wants to prevent Our Lord from suffering; Jesus gives him a rebuke and a correction. Jesus wants to bless children, but the apostles try to keep them away from Him; He tells them: "Let the little ones come to Me, and forbid them not." The mother of the two Zebedees asks Jesus to permit that her two sons should hold the first two places in His kingdom, the one to His right, the other to His left. Our Lord answers: "You know not what you ask." When Mary Magdalene anoints our Saviour in the house of the Pharisee, the apostles get angry and say: "To what purpose is this waste?" Jesus answers: "Why do you trouble this woman?" The disciples quarrel amongst themselves as to who was to be the first and greatest in Christ's kingdom; the Master teaches them that he who would become the lowest in humility would be the highest before God. After His agony in the garden, Jesus returns to His apostles and finds them sleeping. He told them: "Watch and pray, lest you enter into temptation!" and now He says: "What! could you not watch one hour with Me?" Judas betrays his Master; Peter denies Him, in spite of his liveliest attestation of fidelity; the other disciples all forsake Jesus, and run away when He is taken captive by the soldiers; yet Jesus has patience still, and bears with the weakness of His Apostles. This is Jesus, our Model, whom we must follow.

On one special occasion, when Jesus wished to enter the city of Samaria, and the inhabitants refused to receive Him, two of the apostles, James and John, said: "Lord, wilt Thou that we command fire to come down from heaven and consume them?" Jesus answers: "You know not of what spirit you are! The Son of Man came not to destroy souls, but to save!" Do you understand now what is the spirit of Jesus? And will you try, as followers of Jesus, to acquire this spirit for yourselves? "Learn of Me, for I am meek and humble of heart," says our divine Model.

The Saints had this same spirit. They always had great patience with others. Whenever anything happened that was naturally annoying, they let it pass by and took it all quietly. I will give you an example.

St. Ephrem had been fasting for several days, when he told his servant to cook and dish up a mess of vegetables. He was sitting in his room, waiting. The servant comes along, carrying the bowl of cooked vegetables, but, alas! as he enters through the door he stumbles and falls. The bowl is broken to pieces, the mess of vegetables poured out on the floor.

What do you think now? Did the Saint bristle up and get angry? Did he stamp the floor and scold? Did he say: "You confounded simpleton! can't you take more care?" Ah, no! Ephrem was a saint! The servant, poor fellow, turned quite pale from fear, but his master remained quiet, and said in a pleasant tone: "Don't be disturbed, my dear son. Since the pottage will not come to me to be eaten, I must go down to it." And the saint sat down on the floor, and scraping together the spilled vegetables, ate of them as much as he could take up.

You may have to live with children that are cross, and ill-mannered, and hard to get along with; or you may have to reside in a neighborhood where people, grown and children, are very coarse in language and rough in manners; or you may go out into the country to visit your relations; you find the folks, especially the children, so ill-bred and vulgar; in short, you will often have to deal with persons who have all kinds of curious ways and strange manners, hard to get along with. What then?

First: remember that you have your faults, as well as others. You must not expect others to be perfect, or to become so in a short time, when you are far from being perfect yourself. Secondly: if you can do anything to improve your surroundings in ways and manners, you may try it; but do so with a good intention and in the right way. Above all, as the Latin proverb says, " Festina lente," which means in English, "Make haste slowly!" Rome was not built in one day. You will not improve much, neither yourself nor others, if you imagine it all has to be done in one day. Take it slowly. Give yourself and others plenty of time. A spirit of gentleness and patient forbearance will do wonders, whereas rashness and impatience will only spoil and waste.

"Study to be patient," says Thomas à Kempis, "in learning the defects of others, and their infirmities, be they what they may, for thou hast many things which others must bear withal.

XVII.
Vocation.

"THE Following of Christ," in chapter the seventeenth of the first book, treats on the Monastic Life; that is, it tells us how a person must be and what he must do to lead a good and happy life as member of a religious order or community. Instead of speaking to you about religious or monastic life in particular, I wish rather to say a few words about vocation in general.

God calls every person growing up to manhood or womanhood to serve Him in a certain station of life. This calling, which God gives one, as also the station of life that one embraces after perceiving this call, are both called vocation. We pray to God to show us our vocation; and when once he has shown it to us, and we know it, and have entered it according to His holy will, we keep on praying to God that He may assist us constantly with His grace to faithfully serve Him in that vocation, to do His holy will until death.

It is all-important to find out this vocation and to embrace it. If one should happen to enter the wrong vocation—a vocation to which God has not called him—it would be a dreadful misstep, and might prove to be a fatal one. God, in a certain measure, gives His graces according to the vocation He has marked out for one. If you have embraced that station of life to which God has called you, you will receive those special graces He has prepared for you—graces that are necessary to fulfil the duties of your station faithfully and perseveringly, and to overcome bravely the obstacles that you will meet with in your way. If you have embraced the wrong vocation, then, naturally, many of these graces will be wanting, and the difficulties on your way greater.

You must not think, however, that, if you should have chanced to make the misstep, that is, if you have entered the wrong vocation, you must then give yourself up for lost. No, indeed! Never give yourself up for lost. God is always willing, even if you have entered a vocation against His will, to give you all the graces you may stand in need of in order to save your soul in that vocation. But you will meet with and have to overcome greater obstacles, and your work will be a great deal harder. It is like this: instead of taking the straight, smooth road to your home, you have taken a side road, rough, full of logs, stumps, mud-puddles, briars, and thorns; it is a long, roundabout way, hard to travel; but keep on faithfully; even on that road you can still reach your home!

From this you can see how important it is to find out one's vocation, and after having found it, to follow it. How many vocations are there? And what should you do to find out your own?

Vocations may be divided into two classes: Life in the world, and life consecrated to God in religion. Life in the world may be of two kinds: single life, and married life. So, also, life in religion may be of two kinds: the priesthood, and life in a religious order or community, as Brother or Sister.

Of all these different vocations it may not be wrong to assert that that of married life, though not the highest in worth, is yet the most important, on account of the manifold, far-reaching, grave duties connected with it— duties on whose fulfilment both the temporal and eternal welfare of all mankind depend.

Why is it that there is so much misery in family life? that so many families are unhappy, even here in this world, and are doing nothing but making themselves unhappy also for the next? Certainly, there may be many other reasons, different from the one given here ; but in many a case, this may be the first cause of all the subsequent misery : father and mother were not called to enter the married state ; or, they were not called to be partners in that state ; they have entered the wrong vocation.

Thanks to the good God! There are many whom God calls to the holy state of the priesthood, and to a religious life, even in our days. God will never let these vocations die out, if we may say so. But the number of persons living a single life in the world, comparatively, is very small. What do you think? Is the state of single life in the world, consecrated to virginal purity, less pleasing to God than it was hundreds of years ago?

Ah, yes! it is so important to find out one's right vocation.

Then, what should you do to find it out? When the time has come for you to choose a vocation, then do as follows : first, you must see to have yourself instructed in all that is necessary for you to know concerning the various stations of life. Such books as "The

Youth's Director," "Catholic Christian Instructed," and others that might be named, will give you much of the information you may need. For particular instructions apply to the priest, your pastor. Secondly, you must pray much and devoutly to the Holy Ghost. I would especially counsel you to make a novena—nine days' devotion—to the Blessed Virgin, the Mother of Good Counsel. During the devotion try to go to confession and to holy Communion once extra. Thirdly, it will also be good if, in a general confession of your whole life, you will open your heart to a good, learned, and experienced confessor, and let him guide you in this all-important affair.

If you do all this in humility, and with a good will and intention, God will not fail to show you the way. Whatever, then, be your vocation, strike out for it courageously, and hold on to it faithfully.

You must not envy others, who may be called by God to something higher and better than you are. Be you faithful in the little, and you shall have the same reward as those that have been faithful in the great. King David said to his men after the battle with the Amalekites:

"Equal shall be the portion of him who went down to battle, and of him that abode at the baggage : and they shall divide alike."

My little follower of Jesus, this chapter must close now. I would like to wedge in a little story, by way of illustration ; but you must do without it this time. St. Paul admonishes us : " As God hath called every man so let him walk." "A cripple limping in the right way is better than a racer out of it," says St. Augustine. And Thomas à Kempis remarks : " He that seeketh anything else but simply God and the salvation of his soul, will find nothing but trouble and sorrow.

XVIII.

Example of the Saints.

"No man lighteth a candle," says Jesus, "and putteth it in a hidden place, nor under a bushel; but upon a candlestick, that all who come in may see the light."

If you read the lives of the saints, and compare one with the other, you will find that most of them, as in other points, so also agreed in this: They tried to keep their good works secret, to hide the light of holiness that was burning in their lives. The world, frequently, knew them not, made little of them, despised them, persecuted them; so that the wicked, on the Day of Judgment, according to Holy Scripture, will say: "These are they, whom we had sometime in derision, and for a parable of reproach. We fools esteemed their life madness, and their end without honor. Behold, how they are numbered among the children of God, and their lot is among the saints."

But God does not wait till the Day of Judgment to reveal this beautiful light of holiness in His saints. He put many of them on the candlestick even while they were yet living in this world. Do what they would to hide the light, God so disposed that it had to break forth. It shone brightly, and enlightened the darkness of the world round about them. Their example was a silent but powerful sermon, that often did more to draw sinners out of their wickedness and drive them on toward God than the most eloquent missionary could do with all his preaching.

St. Francis of Assisi went out one day with one of his brethren, with the intention, as he said, of preaching a sermon. They passed through the town, one street after another, without, however, saying a single word. The people came out to meet them, not to hear the sermon, but to scoff at them, to load them with insults.

When they returned home, St. Francis asked his companion: "Well, my brother, how did you like my sermon?"

"Father," said the latter, "what shall I say? I heard nothing like a sermon. You did not say even one word."

"Yet we have both preached a good sermon," replied the saint. "By our good example we have taught them how to bear insults patiently and in silence."

Do you see? This is the way the saints all preached.

Sometimes God so ordained that the sanctity of His saints remained hidden to the world as long as they lived; but so much the brighter did the light shine forth after their death. Read your "Lives of the Saints;" there is light in it, and fire.

My dear little follower of Jesus, we all should look up to this light; we should draw near and warm ourselves at this heavenly fire. It is the fire of God's love that burned, and is burning still, in the hearts of His saints. The same fire should burn in our hearts. Let me tell you what you ought to do.

First: you ought to have a "Legend of Saints" in your house. If you have none yet, your parents certainly will get you one as soon as they can, if you ask them. Do not let it lie idle, though; you ought to read in it every day. You ought, at least, to read the life of the saint that is given for each day. Read it carefully, not merely for pastime. Try to find out which is the principal virtue for which the saint was renowned; make up your resolution to imitate it. In this way you will draw great benefit from your reading. The "Lives of the Saints" is the Gospel carried out in practice.

Secondly: there will be a few saints for whom you will feel a special liking. They hold a higher place in your regard and affection than others. Read their lives frequently, and with particular care; and take special pains to imitate their virtues.

Thirdly: you ought to have a book containing, more extensive and complete, the life of the saint whose name you bear. Read that book through often; get it by heart, I might say. Strive to imitate your patron, and you will become, like him, a true follower of Jesus.

Thomas à Kempis says: "They, the holy Fathers, were given for an example to all religious; and ought more to excite us to advance in good than the number of lukewarm induce us to grow remiss."

XIX.

Exercises of a Good Christian.

"THE Following of Christ," in this chapter, treats on "The Exercises of a Good Religious." Our title is a little different in one word. Instead of "Religious" we put "Christian."

If you have the book, or can easily get it, I would advise you, before you proceed any further in reading this, to read that chapter in *The Following of Christ*. It is chapter the nineteenth of book the first. There is so much said there that I cannot repeat here. Read it slowly. Pause after every verse and ponder it. Indeed, it is worth thinking over: every verse—so true—is of more worth than gold!

Now, let us go on. A good Christian means a good follower of Christ. It is your purpose, is it not, to become a good, true follower of Jesus? Then, look ahead! Jesus goes before you: keep up your courage and push on after your Saviour.

Here are a few rules, together with some points of good advice.

First: you must have a constant desire

to become better, to get up nearer to Jesus. You must pray for this desire every day; pray that it may not get weaker, but rather increase in strength from day to day. "This is our life," says St. Augustine: "to make progress in virtue by continual desire." And St. Bernard says: . "He that will not go forward, without doubt begins to go backward."

Secondly: you must not be satisfied with having a general desire for perfection. You ought to have a special good resolution every morning to strive after perfection; to make good use of the means that will help you forward; to avoid all that might hinder you. "As our purpose is," says Thomas à Kempis, "so will our progress be; and there is need of much diligence for him that wisheth to advance much."

Thirdly: with this general desire and special purpose, you must unite those exercises that all good Christians who are earnest about their salvation undertake and perform. First come morning and evening prayers. I hope your parents have introduced it as a rule in the family, and have it observed strictly every day, to say morning and evening prayers together, parents and children. If not, you must do it alone for yourself. You need not expect that you will ever become a true follower of Jesus, unless you are punctual in this, saying your morning and night prayers! Next comes the daily examination of your conscience. Do that in the evening, before you retire to bed. Especially examine yourself as to your prevailing passion, or strongest evil inclination. After the examination, never fail to make an act of contrition. The acts of faith, hope, and charity you might make in the morning, as part of your morning prayers. But do not fail to make them every day.

You should also receive the sacraments—go to confession and holy Communion often,— at least once a month.

Lastly, I would advise you to make a resolution every morning to do something particular that day which will be pleasing to God. Once you might resolve to say certain short, ejaculatory prayers frequently during the day, to keep you mindful of the presence of God; another time you might resolve to mortify your appetite a little, or to guard yourself more carefully against a certain fault, or to keep silence more, or to practise little works of charity, and so on.

See, my children, these are some—only a few—of the exercises of a good Christian. What will you do, then?

You say: "It is so hard to keep one's self always tied down to such practices!" I say so myself; it is a hark task. But just think: what will be your reward one day? A farmer, on his death-bed, called his sons together, and said to them:

"Listen, my children: somewhere on the farm that I leave you there lies hidden in the ground a great treasure. Set to work and hunt for it; if you find it you will be rich." The sons worked diligently. Every year, for a long period, they plow and work their farm in hopes of finding the treasure. Did they find it? Yes; but not as they had expected. The farm, as fruit of the work done on it, produced the richest harvests; and in a few years the brothers were well-to-do. Do you understand the meaning of this parable? and can you make the application?

Pray often with Thomas à Kempis: "Help me, O Lord God, in my good purpose, and in Thy holy service; and grant that I may this day begin indeed, since what I have hitherto done is nothing."

XX.

Silence and Solitude.

"SET a watch, O Lord, before my mouth, and a door round about my lips!"

Thus prays the Psalmist. In the words of this short prayer there lies hidden a thought which it would be well for us to consider. Let us draw it forth:

David does not ask God to lock up and seal his lips, nor to build up a wall before his mouth, that he might never break through with his tongue to speak even a single word, good or bad. No! he asks God to give him the grace always to make good use of his tongue, that he might speak only what is useful and edifying, and avoid by silence what might be harmful; that he might open his lips to speak, and close them in silence, at the right time, just as one would open and close the door of a house or room. This is the thought: isn't it an excellent one?

Holy Scripture says, somewhere else: "There is a time to keep silence, and a time to speak." God does not wish us to be silent all the time. He gave us our tongues that we might use them also for talking, but we are allowed to speak only what is good, and at the right time.

Indeed, if God had so willed, he could easily have made our tongues so that we could never have used them for speaking, neither for good nor for bad—you know how the brutes are in this respect.

Here is an example that I read in a book some time ago: St. Vincent Ferreri was one day preaching in the street in the beautiful old city of Valencia. During his sermon a woman who is dumb is brought before him. He sees the poor creature's good will and strong faith: is it God's will that she should receive the gift of speech?

The Saint halts in his sermon a few minutes and raises his heart to God in ardent prayer, after which he turns to the woman and asks: "What is it you would like to have, my daughter?"

"Bread, and the use of my tongue!" answers the woman, loudly and distinctly. On beholding the miracle, the people burst out into a cry of joy and admiration. They praise and glorify God for His goodness.

"Bread you shall have, my daughter, as long

as you live," continues the Saint. "God will not let you suffer again from want of food. But the use of your tongue it is not His will to give you. He foresees that by using it you would commit many sins: your tongue would be sharper than a sword—it would cut, and wound, and do much harm; in the end it would bring eternal ruin to your soul. Hence, my daughter, be satisfied with God's holy will. You shall be dumb as you have been heretofore, to the end of your life."

The woman signifies her willingness. She was never heard to speak again until she died.

My little followers of Jesus, to most of us God has given the free use of the tongue: we can speak. But, God has also given us His law. He tells us clearly and definitely what we are allowed to speak, and what not.

He has also given us reason and conscience; we know what is good and bad—reason shows us, conscience tells us. We know also what is good and bad in speaking. Furthermore, God helps us with His grace to keep His law faithfully; He will also help us not to sin by speaking. Do you understand now why Jesus says so strictly: "I say unto you, that every idle word that men shall speak, they shall render an account for it in the Day of Judgment"?

We can never be true followers of Jesus unless we learn to govern our tongues; Thomas à Kempis has already given us several lessons on this; now he says: "He that aims at inward and spiritual things must, with Jesus, turn aside from the crowd." Do you understand what this means? It is not enough for us to guard our tongues, so that they may not say what is wrong, or say things at the wrong time. We must withdraw from company altogether, sometimes; we must tie our tongues and keep them silent—in a word, we must strive to acquire a love for solitude and silence.

We have the example of Jesus for this. "Jesus went up into the mountain alone to pray," says St. Matthew. And this the holy Gospel tells us, in the same or similar words, more than once. Shall we not try to follow the example that Jesus gives us?

Remember, therefore, these points: First, whenever duty keeps you at home, away from company or your playmates, then be satisfied. Do not grumble, or complain inwardly. Yes, you ought to be glad. Now you can do something to acquire a love for solitude and silence.

Turn your thoughts to God; think that He is present. If you have any work to do, do it faithfully. If you have none to do, look for some. You must not idle away your time. If you can find nothing to do, then, at least, take up a good book and read it. Do not fret, and keep thinking of your playmates—what they are doing, the fun they are having, and so on.

Secondly, it is left to your choice frequently; you may go out into company, or not, just as you like. You might, sometimes, choose to stay at home, for the love of Jesus, to mortify yourself by keeping silence. I know, children must have recreation. But you must not be talking, and laughing, and jumping, and running about, and playing, and having fun all the time, what do you think? Is that the way Jesus did? Hence deny yourself once in a while. When you might go out into company, retire and keep silence.

The Following of Christ says: "It is easier to keep silence altogether, than not to fall into excess in speaking; easier to keep retired at home than to be enough upon one's guard abroad."

XXI.

Sorrow of Heart.

"IT is wonderful," says Thomas à Kempis, "that any man can ever abandon himself wholly to joy in this life, when he considereth and weigheth his exile and the dangers of his soul."

Represent to yourself Jesus, your model. Can you think of him as laughing immoderately, breaking out into fits of unusual mirth, as we are sometimes apt to do? No. We behold our Saviour, both as a child, and as a grown man, always steady, earnest, and quiet. He was meek, friendly, and full of the most winning love, certainly; but withal, His countenance ever wore an expression of thoughtful earnestness, and His outward manner, though calm and gentle, bespoke a certain mournfulness of spirit. The gospels nowhere tell us that Jesus laughed, or even smiled; but we read that He wept now and then, maybe, frequently. He had a great work to perform—to suffer and die for the redemption of mankind; and yet He knew that, in spite of His efforts to save them, so many, very many, would be lost forever. Hence, that sorrow of His heart, those tears He shed.

It well becomes a follower of Jesus, therefore, to be sorrowful of heart. Yes, our Lord even gives this as one of the signs by which we can tell whether or not we are His followers. "Blessed are they that mourn; for they shall be comforted." And to His apostles He says —words, as it were, expressing His bequest to them: "Amen, amen, I say to you, that you shall lament and weep; but the world shall rejoice."

However, you must understand this aright. It is not said that you must always keep your spirit under pressure; that you must always mourn, and sigh, and weep; that you dare never be cheerful, dare never laugh, nor play, nor enjoy yourself in any way. Holy Scripture says: "There is a time to weep, and a time to laugh." And *The Following of Christ*, speaking to us about the sorrow we ought to have in our hearts, tells us, in the same chapter, where we can find true liberty and joy— "in the fear of God with a good conscience." What should you do, therefore?

In your dealings with others you must try to be kind, cheerful, and, as we would say, gentlemanly. Your looks, your features, all your actions should be such as to express the kindness and charity of your heart. Take care, also, not to go to extremes, never to be wantonly gay, nor unduly sorrowful.

But for yourself, you must also cultivate a spirit of holy earnestness and sorrow of heart —in which Jesus sets such a good example. What are the motives that might tend to make us earnest-minded and sorrowful of heart? There are plenty of such motives.

Consider, for instance, the misery of this world. Bodily, we are subject to sickness and pains and troubles of every kind. The greatest and last misery in this world is death. As to our souls, there are so many dangers and temptations to sin; the enemies that hate us and try to bring us to ruin are so watchful and cunning—you know we are never sure, even for one moment, but we may lose God, our souls, heaven, everything. Wherever we turn our eyes, wee see so much wickedness, so much misery caused by sin—the poor oppressed by the rich, the righteous persecuted by the unjust. Who must not feel sad at heart, who would not rather sigh and weep than laugh and be joyful, when he sees and considers all this misery?

Dionysius, the tyrant of Syracuse, one day invited a certain man, named Damocles, to come to his palace and be a guest at his table. Damocles had tried by flatteries to gain the king's favor. He had praised him greatly for his wisdom and justice, extolled his power and riches, and therefore he hoped the king would reward him by making him one of the first officers in his kingdom. You may imagine what were the man's expectations when the king sent him this invitation.

Damocles came. First he had to change his clothes: he was clad in the finest, richest garments, like the king himself. Then he was led into the large dining hall, where he was given a place next to the king. The table was loaded with victuals and beverages most costly and delicious—more than ever he could have imagined or desired. Besides, he was honored by the other guests and servants as if he were the king's own brother. Damocles was happy for once: yes, a regular sea of happiness, he thought it!

In the midst of his pleasure, however, there comes a sudden terror. He just happens, once, to raise his eyes to the ceiling. What is the matter? He turns pale; he can eat no more, nor drink; he trembles in all the limbs of his body.

There, right above his head, hangs a sharp, heavy sword; it hangs on a horsehair, only a horsehair! If the hair breaks the sword will fall and split his head.

"Do you see now, Damocles, what it is to be king? I am not safe for one hour; any moment death and ruin may overtake me," said Dionysius.

This, my dear little follower of Jesus, is a picture of the vain and sinful joys of the world.

XXII.

Human Misery.

SOLOMON, you know, was a mighty king. If any one could speak of happiness on this earth, certainly he could; for, says he: "I surpassed in riches all that were before me in Jerusalem. Whatsoever my eyes desired, I refused them not: and I withheld not my heart from enjoying every pleasure." But in the end he confesses: "I have seen all things that are done under the sun: and, behold, all is vanity and vexation of spirit."

You know also the history of Job. Well, here are some of his words: "The life of man upon earth is a warfare. If I be wicked, woe unto me; and if just, I shall not lift up my head, being filled with affliction and misery. Oh, that I had been consumed, that eye might not see me!"

A rich man had two grown sons. One day he called them to his room and said:

"My sons, listen. I will give each of you an equal portion of land to work on my farm. I am getting old, and am going to leave things more for you to manage. Be diligent in your work; be saving, and do not lose time. Bring me your profits; I will treasure them up for you; and sometime you will receive your reward from me accordingly."

There was a great difference between these two brothers. The older was a good son, obedient and respectful. He was not afraid to work; and from his earliest childhood he had tried to learn what might be necessary and useful for a farmer to know. He was able now to work the farm, and manage it successfully. Not so the younger. He was indolent and careless, and thus caused his father much trouble. He was afraid to work; he tried every means to avoid it. It was thus he had grown up. He knew very little about farming, and did not care to know more.

The older brother worked his land well. He manured it, and plowed, and harrowed, and sowed. He worked hard; it cost him many a drop of sweat; often he was nearly tired out. But for this he had good harvests; and how glad he was when each autumn he could lay a good sum of money in his father's hand. Not so did the younger brother. He was afraid to work the land himself; he hired others. These cared little about the harvests, if only they got their wages. His land was just as good as his brother's; but instead of improving it lost in value. His harvests were poor; and they became poorer every year. After he had paid the wages to his hired men he had very little left to give as profits to his father. After two or three years he had no profits at all to give.

Thus it went on for ten years. The father died. The testament he had made was an unexpected surprise, He left all his property to his two sons, to be divided between them proportionally, according to the amount of profits each one had brought to his father during those ten years they had been left the management of that land. The younger son got—just one acre of land. The older inherited all the rest—the great riches of his father. The younger son was enraged: he stamped and scolded. But, had he good reason to do so? Wasn't he treated right?

My dear little followers of Jesus, this is a parable from which we can learn a good lesson. Let us hear:

We are not created for this world. Jesus died for us to redeem us; He wants to have us with Him in heaven, forever. For He says:

"Where I am, there also shall My servant be." Now, if this world were all sweetness, if there were nothing bitter in it, we might like it too much; we might forget the home and happiness that are awaiting us in eternity.

"Oh, unfortunate mankind!" exclaims St. Augustine. "The world is bitter, and yet it is loved. Imagine how much more it would be loved if it were sweet." And Thomas à Kempis says: "Some there are who cling to the world so closely (though even by laboring or by begging they hardly have bare necessaries) that, could they live here always, they would care nothing for the kingdom of God."

Can you make out now why there is so much misery in the world?

I will not weary you with an account of the manifold afflictions that may fall upon us in this life. You might, for this, read the corresponding chapter in *The Following of Christ*—chapter twenty-second of book first. I will only say this: you are still young, and have not yet experienced any or but very little of the misery of this world. But it will come for you also, this experience, sooner or later. We are all children of Adam; and we all come under Adam's sentence of judgment: "Cursed is the earth in thy work! Thorns and thistles shall it bring forth to thee." As often as you have to feel this misery, think of the two brothers. Now is your time of hard work: the harvest of reward will be accordingly. I must add a word from Thomas à Kempis: "When thou art troubled and afflicted, then is the time of merit. Thou must pass through fire and water before thou come to refreshment."

XXIII.

Thoughts on Death.

THE last few chapters we have gone through were such as to awaken in us very earnest thoughts. Life is earnest; as followers of Jesus it becomes us to take an earnest view of it. And here, now, comes a chapter on death! Do not be frightened, my little reader. You must die once, as well as I; hence these few thoughts on death are for you just as well as they are for me. To introduce them, let me tell you a short story.

A merchant and a sailor once got into a friendly conversation. Amongst other things the merchant asks: "Pray, tell me, my friend, what kind of a death did your father have?"

"My father, like my grandfather and great-grandfather before him, died by drowning in the sea," replied the sailor.

"And you still venture to go out on the sea? Are you not afraid that you, also, shall have to die by drowning, some day?"

"No. Why should I be afraid? Tell me, what kind of a death did your father, grandfather, and great-grandfather die?" asks the sailor in turn.

"They all died in their beds," answered the merchant.

"Do you see, now," remarked the sailor. "Why should I be more afraid to go to sea, than you are to go to bed?"

From this, we can collect the following thoughts: though it is uncertain when, and where, and how we shall die, it is quite certain—nothing, indeed, more certain—that once we have to die, each and every one of us. As sure as you live, you will have to die. Impress this thought on your mind and heart; the angel of death stands on your way; you cannot escape him!

You are young and healthy, but who knows? will you have your health long? Will you grow old? God only knows that. You can hurry on Death, so that he will cut you off sooner, but you cannot keep him away so that he will never come.

A certain child, once, was reported to have died. Somebody went to the house to see if the report was true.

"My child dead!" said the father, laughing, "That's funny! The boy is as well as I am.

Come in, and see for yourself. Ha! ha! That's a good sign, anyhow; people say that when one is reported dead this way, he will surely have a long and happy life."

But people's saying doesn't help. When it is time for Death to come, he comes, and no one can keep him away. That child died only a few weeks later. The boy was taken sick suddenly, and in a few hours he was a corpse.

There is a life after death—an eternal life. This is certain. As sure as Jesus, our Saviour, rose from the grave and is living again, so sure is it that we, too, must rise from the grave again one day, then to live, body and soul united, for an eternity. Our lot will be an eternity, either of happiness or misery, and this lot, remember, depends on the kind of life we lead now, and the kind of death we shall die once.

We do not want to be foolish, do we? No; we want to act wisely. Jesus says: "Blessed are those servants whom the Lord, when he cometh, shall find watching." And *The Following of Christ* remarks: "How happy and how prudent is he who now striveth to be in life what he would fain be found in death!"

Hence, you must avoid sin, now and as long

as you live. You must neither dare to commit mortal sin, nor live in it for one hour. Death might overtake you suddenly; then, what? "Behold! I come as a thief. Blessed is he that watcheth!"

Correct your bad habits; now is the time! Do not carry them with you all through life. If you bring them with you to your deathbed, they will press heavily on your heart. They will be thorns in your pillow, tormenting you in your dying hour.

Do your good works now, for "the night cometh, when no man can work." Say your prayers every day; go to the sacraments often; attend divine service faithfully on Sundays and holydays; take pains to hear, read, and meditate on the Word of God; be charitable according to the means which God has given you. Thomas à Kempis admonishes: "Study so to live, that, in the hour of death, thou mayest be able rather to rejoice than to fear."

Above all, do everything with a good intention. You know how, for you have often been told. It is very important—this good intention. May Jesus help us, and the Blessed Virgin pray for us, that we may not, at the end of our lives, have to exclaim, with St. Peter: "We have labored all night, and have taken nothing." These are the few "Thoughts on Death," I tried to gather for you into this chapter.

For the conclusion, the first verse of Longfellow's "Psalm of Life:"

> Life is real! Life is earnest!
> And the grave is not its goal;
> Dust thou art, to dust returnest,
> Was not spoken of the soul.

And a word from Thomas à Kempis: "Blessed is the man that hath the hour of his death continually before his eyes, and daily putteth himself in order for death."

XXIV.

Judgment and what comes after.

OUR last end is one of these two : heaven or hell. There is no other alternative. Either we shall be forever happy with God, the angels, and saints, in heaven ; or we shall be miserable for all eternity with the devils and damned in hell. Our first end is the service of God now, while we are living on earth. We are created to know, love, and serve God. By doing this faithfully—striving after our first end—we do what is necessary to reach our last end. It all depends on knowing, loving, and serving God well, now. Let us not forget this.

Our working for heaven ends with death. "When the tree falleth, to the north or to the south, in what place soever it shall fall, there shall it be." After death comes the judgment. "It is appointed for men once to die, and after this, the judgment," says St. Paul. This thought of the judgment, my dear children, must engage our·attention for a few minutes. *The Following of Christ* admonishes us: "In all things look to the end, and how thou wilt stand before the strict Judge, from whom there is nothing hid; who takes no bribes, and receives no excuses, but will judge that which is just."

Three young men, once upon a time, were making a journey. They were in the holy land of Palestine, and on their way they came to the valley of Josaphat.

"Hold, comrades!" said one of them—a light-headed infidel, "here, they say, is where the Last Judgment is going to be. Priests talk so much about it, I guess, as I am here just now, I will look for a handy place to sit, so that, when the Day of Judgment is come I may have a good chance to take in everything, and see what is going on. Here is an excellent place—a stone to mark it. I can sit on this stone and have a clear view over the whole valley. This shall be my place."

And he laughed, he thought the idea was so original; and his two companions laughed with him.

But something happened. That same moment the young man had a vision. He saw Jesus Christ, the Judge; and terrible was His appearance, terrible the majesty of that divine countenance, terrifying the look of anger that fell upon the young man. It makes him tremble; he grows pale as death; he staggers and falls to the ground; and there he lies, unconscious. After a time his companions succeeded in waking him.

"What is the matter? What has happened?" they ask.

He sighs; he weeps; he still trembles violently. "Oh, comrades, it was terrible! I saw the Judge! That look! Let us never make fun of the Judgment again."

And the story concludes by telling us that the young man never made fun again. He never even laughed. Till his death he led a severe life of penance.

Ah, yes; it is a terrible thought—this judgment! My little followers of Jesus, after death we shall all be judged. You will stand alone before your Judge. It is no longer the kind, meek, and humble Jesus. Now He is the strict Judge, who knows only justice. And you must answer for yourself, alone. The Judge knows all—all the good and bad that you did in thought, word, and action during your life on earth. The sentence will be one or the other. If you come as the friend of Jesus, you will hear: "Come, thou blessed one!" but if you stand before the Judge as His enemy, He will say: "Depart from Me, thou accursed one!" Oh, this sentence, what will it be!

The Last Day of Judgment will come; also. Then you will have to stand on one side or the other, either the right or the left. Then you will be judged again before all men: they will see both the good and the bad that you have done; and they will all have to say: "Thy judgments, O Lord, are just!" And then you will hear the sentence again—one of the two, the same that was spoken to you immediately after your death. And then comes the beginning of your last end—either an everlasting heaven, or an everlasting hell. This, my children, is truth: we cannot gainsay it!

Should we not, then, prepare ourselves for this judgment? Yes; let us judge ourselves now, that we may be able to stand the judgment then. Let us avoid sin now. If we have sinned (unfortunately we have!) let us confess our sins, and do penance for them; on the Last Day it will be too late. Let us do good now, for then we shall be able to work no longer. Let us suffer now, that we may not have to suffer then. Let us receive the sacraments often while we can, and worthily, lest we shall wish to have done so when it is too late.

"In all thy works remember thy last end, and thou shalt never sin," says the Holy Ghost. To this add a word from Thomas à Kempis: "He that loveth God with his whole heart feareth neither death, nor punishment, nor judgment, nor hell; for perfect love giveth secure access to God."

XXV.
Amend Your Life.

WE now come to chapter the twenth-fifth, and that closes the first book of *The Following of Christ*. Let us hold a short review of what we have gone through so far; it will freshen things a little in our memories.

We began by laying out the road for you. Your intention is to be a follower of Jesus: then, walk after your Saviour, who goes before you, and take care lest you be misled by the vain, deceitful promises of the world.

The foundation you must build on is humility. Thomas à Kempis lays great stress on this. He treats on this virtue in an extra chapter; and off and on, all through the first book, he calls our attention to it. We need not imagine that we will ever become true followers of Jesus, unless we strive to be humble. Let us not forget this.

You need a teacher and guide; Jesus Himself wants to be both for you. You remember yet, I suppose, what you were told about the different ways in which Jesus can speak to us.

Jesus teaches you, and He confirms His

doctrine by giving you His own example, that, besides humility, the fundamental virtue, there are some other virtues you must try earnestly to acquire and practise—prudence, mortification, obedience, patience, chastity, love for solitude, silence, and a wholesome sorrow of heart. There are particular faults you must guard against: avoid evil companions, watch your tongue, do not judge rashly, and so on.

Some of the means that you must use to perfect yourself—to acquire the above-named virtues, and to avoid the faults mentioned—are the following: good reading, spiritual guidance from a good confessor, being watchful, so as to resist every temptation in the very beginning, imitation of the saints, faithfulness in the performance of your daily prayers and religious exercises, and lastly, frequent meditation on our last end death, judgment, heaven, hell. One very important thing is : you must pray much, even now, that God may point out to you your vocation, and lead you into it, and that He may keep you from entering a wrong one. So much for the repetition.

Our Lord says to His disciples: "Amen, I say unto you, unless you be converted, and become as little children, you shall not enter into the kingdom of heaven." Must we not all confess that we are very far from being like little children? It is necessary for us, therefore, to convert ourselves; and what a work that will be for most of us!

How good, how innocent, how holy is such a child—one in whose heart the grace and love of God dwell, and on which the blight sin has not yet fallen! St. Hilary, one of the holy Fathers, may tell us how such a child is, and what it does: "The child," he says, "obeys its father, loves its mother, knows nothing of ill-will against its neighbor; it cares not for riches; it does not show itself proud, neither does it bear hatred, nor tell lies; it believes what others say, and takes as true what it hears."

Well, then, my little followers of Christ, shall we not set to work earnestly to change and amend our lives? Yes, certainly. Here are a few points we must try to remember: —

First: we must study our own natures—mortify ourselves in what we are unduly inclined to, and strive after the good we stand most in need of. Secondly: We should imitate the good we see in others and avoid carefully what does not please us in their ways and actions. Thirdly: again and again we must set Jesus before our eyes, to meditate on His life, and to imitate Him. "Whosoever," says Thomas à Kempis, "exerciseth himself earnestly and devoutly in the most holy life and passion of our Lord, shall find there abundantly all that is necessary and useful for him; nor need he seek out of Jesus for anything better."

Fourthly: we must frequently renew our good resolutions. We must not lose courage when we find sometimes that we have forgotten them, and, therefore, have fallen back into our old faults. We must be sorry for what we have done, and make our resolution over again —not lightly, carelessly, but considerately, and in earnest.

There was a boy once who was very careless. He was good-hearted, yet he gave his parents much trouble. Often they corrected and admonished him; and he promised to do better, promised sincerely. But he was naturally so careless that his promises were soon forgotten.

One day, as he was skipping about the room, he bumped his head against a large, costly picture hanging on the wall, and knocked it down. The noise brought his father in, and the little boy was terribly frightened.

"Such carlessness! You only make promises to break them!" exclaimed the father.

"Forgive me this once, dearest father," said the boy, weeping. "I will never be careless again. Let me get a hammer to drive the nail in; and then I will hang up the picture again."

The boy brought the hammer, and having given the nail a few blows with it, he wanted to hang up the picture.

"This carelessness again!" said the father. "Whatever you do, you do only lightly, superficially. Shall the picture fall down again?" And he took the hammer himself, and drove in the nail with many strong blows, till it stuck fast in the wall. "The same must be done with your good resolutions and promises as was done with this nail," remarked the father. "If they are to stick and hold tight, they must be driven deep into your heart. Pray to God; He will help you to strike the blows." Do you see, dear children? It is thus we ought to make our good resolutions.

Lastly, we should often consider: the work is difficult, it is true, but let us persevere. A great reward will come hereafter. "Thou shalt labor a little now," says Thomas à Kempis, " and thou shalt find great rest, yea, everlasting joy."

I conclude with another passage from *The Following of Christ*: "Watch over thyself, stir up thyself, admonish thyself, and whatever may become of others, neglect not thyself. In proportion as thou dost violence to thyself, the greater progress wilt thou make. Amen."

Book Second.

STEPS TOWARDS JESUS.

I.

Interior Life.

IN the "Our Father" Jesus teaches us to pray: "Thy kingdom come." We ask God to grant that His kingdom, the holy Catholic Church, may be spread more and more over the earth, for the salvation of mankind. Not only that; we also pray that His grace and love may ever be in ourselves; that He, our God, our Father and King, may ever reign in our hearts.

Jesus says in another place: "The kingdom of God is within you." Therefore, if God hears our prayer, and lets His kingdom come to us, where will we find it? In our hearts. When once our hearts, through the grace of God, are free from all that is sinful—free from self-love, free from attachment to the world and its vain pleasures; when they are virtuous and holy, filled with burning love for God and our neighbor: then we can say that the kingdom of God is within us.

How happy we shall then be! A happiness will then be ours—true happiness of heart—such as the children of the world cannot have an idea of. St. Paul tells us: "The kingdom of God is not meat and drink; but justice, and peace, and joy in the Holy Ghost."

A father, with his three children, was sitting out in the yard under the shade-giving branches of a maple-tree. He was telling them how all men were striving so earnestly for happiness, but that only so very few really and truly obtain it.

"I believe," said Emma, the youngest, "that beauty alone can bring true happiness. If I am beautiful of person, and do all I can to bring out my beauty and let it shine before men, then I shall be esteemed and admired, and I can get all that I want. But if I am ugly of appearance men will despise me, and I must always feel miserable."

"I don't agree with you," said George, the next older. "Beauty is too easily destroyed. The least attack of sickness, and it may be gone. And if not, how long does it last? A few years, and beauty withers like a flower. I say, money is the thing! Give me money, and I am happy. If I am rich I can get everything I wish for. Money rules the world!"

"What good will beauty and riches do me

if I have not wisdom?" asked Conrad, the oldest. "Give me wisdom, and I shall be happy without beauty or money. But if I am stupid, a block-head, who will care about me? how can I be happy? Now, papa, tell us, which of us is right?"

The father bent down, and with his finger wrote three naughts—000—in the dust.

"What do you mean by that, papa?" asked the children.

"I mean that beauty is a naught, as also are money and wisdom—all three nothing more than three naughts, unless you put some figure before them that has value. The one thing necessary is the love of God, a virtuous heart. Put that one thing before the three naughts of beauty, riches, and wisdom, and you have a large figure of real worth, which signifies real happiness. Take that one thing necessary away, and you have the three naughts—nothing."

Do you see, my dear children? If we want to possess real, true happiness, let us strive to become virtuous. As Thomas à Kempis admonishes, let us "slight exterior things, and give ourselves to interior things, and we shall see the kingdom of God come within us." Let us make our hearts free from the world. Let us not put our confidence in men; let us trust in Jesus! Let us often meditate on the sufferings and death of our dearest Saviour. Let us endeavor to model our hearts after the Heart of Jesus, until we can say: "I live now, not I; but Christ liveth in me." This is interior life! This interior life, hidden, as it were, in Jesus, brings true, lasting happiness. May Jesus bless us, and the Holy Ghost fill our hearts with the light of His grace!

I close this chapter with a passage from *The Following of Christ* · "Come, then, faithful soul, make thy heart ready for this Spouse, so that He may vouchsafe to come to thee and to dwell within thee. For so He sayeth: "If any man love Me, he will keep My Word, and My Father will love him; and We will come to him, and make Our abode with him."

II.
Humble Submission.

WE are much and can do much; we are nothing and can do nothing. Both of these words are true. How so? Understand it this way: Through God's grace we are much, with His help we can do much. Without God we are nothing; without His help we can do nothing. So you see, it all depends on God. With Isaiah, we must say: "All flesh is grass, and all the glory thereof as the flower of the field. The grass is withered, and the flower is fallen." But again, with David, we can say: "The Lord is my Helper: and I will look over my enemies."

A little anecdote may help you to understand this truth better. Albert was out in the granary with his father, holding up the sacks to be filled with wheat. Once, just for a few moments, he was not paying attention as he should have done. The sack was already half filled. His father had just begun to pour in the third half-bushel of wheat. Albert's thoughts had gone travelling: they were on the way to his uncle's, where he was to spend a few days' visit the next week. His fingers loosen their hold on the sack only a little, and, behold! the sack slips from them and falls to the floor. The wheat, instead of going into the sack, is poured out beside it.

A sharp box on the ear from his father, accompanied by a few sharp words of reproof, bring back the boy's straying thoughts. "What are you about, little fellow? Look here; pay attention, and hold up the sack right!"

"Excuse me, papa!" said Albert. "I was just beginning to think about my visit to uncle Joe, next week. I will not let the sack fall again."

Now, for the application. Before God every one of us is even less than an empty sack. All that we are—body and soul, with all our bodily and spiritual qualities and abilities—all is a pure gift of God's love and mercy. Just as the almighty power of God holds and preserves the whole, mighty universe, so He also holds us, every one of us, body and soul, in His almighty hand. If He should let go His hold of us? if He should let us fall? An empty sack, if you let go your hold of it, falls to the ground. We, if God should, even for a moment, let go

His hold of us, would fall down, way down into—nothing! Do you see now, and understand, how completely we are in the hand of God?

This we must not forget. The thought of this, often recalled to our minds, will make us both humble and courageous. It will make us humble: We know and feel that without God we are nothing. If God does not keep us, and help us by His grace, we shall be worse than nothing; we shall be most unfortunate, miserable creatures forever.

This thought will make us courageous; we fear God and nothing else. Are we not in His hand? Is He not an almighty God? Is He not our best, most loving Father? "Can a woman forget her infant, so as not to have pity on her son? and if she should forget, yet will I not forget thee." What, then, shall we fear? Sickness? Poverty? The calumnies, enmities, persecutions of men? Shall we fear death? No! we fear nothing and nobody but God, as our Saviour Himself admonishes us to do: "Be not afraid of them that kill the body, and after that have no more that they can do. But I will show you whom ye shall fear: fear ye Him who, after He hath killed, hath power to cast into hell."

Therefore, my little followers of Jesus, take this thought—a grand, beautiful thought—and treasure it up in your hearts: I am altogether in the hand of God. He supports me, and keeps me from falling, just as one supports a sack while it is being filled with wheat. While God thus supports me He is continually pouring into me His gifts—the most precious gifts of His grace and love. He wants to fill me with treasures for heaven. Oh, if ever He should let me fall! I must love Him, my dearest God—love Him always, love Him ardently. I dare never offend Him by grievous sin. I will pray every day, with St. Philip Neri: "Hold me, O Lord, lest I fall and betray Thee!" I will always do as St. Peter says: "Be you humbled under the mighty hand of God."

But, again, I will not fear; for I trust in the almighty power of my Father in heaven. "If God be for us, who is against us?" Often will I pray, with holy David: "I have put my trust in Thee, O Lord: I said: Thou art my God. My lots are in Thy hands."

Think over this word of Thomas à Kempis: "Make no great account of who may be for or against thee, but mind and take care that God be with thee in everything thou dost."

III.
A Peaceful Disposition.

HOW true are the following words of Thomas à Kempis: "Some there are who keep themselves in peace, and have peace also with others; and there are some who neither have peace themselves, nor leave others in peace; they are troublesome to others, and still more troublesome to themselves."

Just such a one was Fridolin, the hired man of a certain farmer. He had a very quick temper; at everything that did not go just as he wished, he would fly into a passion. Then you should have seen and heard him—how he fumed, and stamped, and scolded; how he quarreled with his fellow-servants, and called them names. He was, therefore, a man very hard to get along with. People were glad not to have much to do with him.

His master often corrected him for it, and admonished him: "Fridolin, you must try to become master of yourself. You should not let it go on this way. You are very passionate; and you thereby commit many sins. The longer you let it go, the harder it will be for you to tear out this evil passion of anger. You know anger is a very disagreeable passion, besides. It never leaves you any rest; and it ever gets you into trouble with others."

Fridolin's answer generally was: "How am I to help it? If they provoke me, or something does not go right, I must get angry. It is just impossible for me to keep cool and quiet."

One morning the farmer showed Fridolin a new silver dollar.

"Look here," said he, "if you are man enough to keep down your anger to-day, so that you wont say an angry word, nor do anything in anger, I will give you this dollar extra besides your wages. Try it. I am pretty sure you wont win."

"I'm pretty sure I will win," thought Fridolin. And so he did. The other servants made out among themselves that they would tease him all day long, and trouble and plague him as much as possible, to see whether they could not get him angry, so that he would say at least an angry word. Their efforts were in vain. Fridolin mastered himself; he was bound to win the dollar.

When evening came, and the work was done, the farmer gave Fridolin the money, and at the same time he said: "Don't you think you ought to feel ashamed of yourself? For the sake of such a miserable bit of money, and to win it, you can keep down your anger, in spite of all that others may do to rouse you into a passion. But for the love of God, and the sake of your soul, you cannot overcome your angry passions."

Fridolin felt that this was true, and was heartily ashamed of himself. He went to work in earnest; so it was not many years before he had become an example of kindness and meekness.

Let us not forget: If sometimes, or often, we get into trouble with our neighbors, if we quarrel with them, and say bitter, harsh words, that make them as well as ourselves feel very unhappy, then we must blame no one but ourselves. It is the "I"—first personal pronoun, nominative case,—that likes to get us into such trouble once in a while.

To acquire a peaceful disposition you must begin on yourself—begin to train the selfish, all-important " I." Jesus says with beautiful meaning, "Have salt in you, and have peace among you."

Put a pinch of salt in your mouth; it does not taste pleasant at all. But put it in what you are cooking, and getting ready to eat: the salt makes it taste very good. So also in a spiritual sense. Mortify yourself, humble your pride, overcome your anger, govern your tongue, guard your actions, etc. This, you feel, is not pleasant—it is the salt of self-mortification. But just keep on; in the same degree that you make progress in this mastering of yourself, in that same degree will you spread joy, and peace, and happiness amongst others.

First, endeavor always to live in peace with God. "Much peace have they who love Thy law," says the Psalmist, "and to them there is no stumbling-block."

Secondly, try to get peace in your own heart. Do as *The Following of Christ* says: "Have a zeal in the first place over thyself, and then mayest thou also justly exercise zeal toward thy neighbor."

Thirdly, along with this, you must try to live in peace with your neighbors. "Cast first the beam out of thine own eye," and "A mild answer breaketh wrath;" if you practise these two things you will do a great deal towards keeping up peace amongst your neighbors.

Another word from Thomas à Kempis to conclude with: "He who best knows how to endure will possess the greater peace. Such a one is a conqueror of himself, and lord of the world, the friend of Christ, and an heir of heaven."

IV.

A Pure Mind and Simple Intention.

"BY two things," says *The Following of Christ*, "is man lifted above earthly things, viz., by simplicity and purity. Simplicity must be in the intention, purity in the affection."

"What kind of birds are those, papa?" asked a little girl of her father, as they were going across a meadow.

"Those birds are called buzzards," answered the father.

"How nicely they are soaring in a ring, and how quietly they fly! One cannot see them move their wings."

"See, how they are gradually lowering themselves toward that forest. Pretty soon they will have reached the tops of the trees."

"What are they coming down for? do they want to rest in the trees?"

"Sometimes they may want to rest," replied the father; "but generally it is not for that purpose that they come down. God created these birds to be very useful. Wherever the buzzards find the carcass of an animal, they will settle down on it to eat it up. Generally a half dozen or more will gather to devour the carrion together. From this you can judge of what great benefit the buzzard is to us. Those seven or eight we have just seen are now probably engaged at this work—eating up the putrid remains of some animal."

Like the buzzard or the eagle, my dear little followers of Jesus, we ought to soar up on high, and raised thus above the earth and all that is earthly, keep moving in the pure atmosphere of God's love. That is, our minds must be pure; our hearts must be free from all inordinate affection for the world or for ourselves.

Oh, yes, most certainly we all desire this— to be thus soaring high up in God's love, with pure hearts, unsullied by sin. We often wish we could sit on top of some light, floating cloud, and thus from on high look down upon the bogs and swamps, deserts and wastes, and the beautiful countries, towns, and cities, rivers, seas, and lakes of the earth. But, alas, we are kept tied down to the earth. Here we must work, eat, drink, and sleep away one third of our life, more or less. Like the buzzard that soars down from its airy height to do the lowest thing even a brute can do—feed on carrion, so we sometimes feel as if we were drawn down from the blissful height of God's love and friendship to the mean and contemptible things of the earth.

But patience, my dear readers! We cannot go away from the earth yet, not until God calls us. We must work, eat, drink, and sleep, and suffer trials and harships for many years yet, perhaps; God wants it so. And here now is where the simplicity of intention comes in. We must do as St. Paul says: "Whether you eat or drink, or whatsoever else you do, do all things for the glory of God." This must be our "simple intention." While we are in this world and must busy ourselves with it, we must, as St. Paul says again, "use this world as if we used it not;" that is, we must not let ourselves be attached to it, so as to forget God and our eternal salvation.

You know there are so many, very many, who do this. They live only for this world, as if they had to stay here forever. Some think only of eating and drinking; when they are done with breakfast they speak already of dinner; hardly have they finished dinner when they already think and make plans about supper. Others there are who live only for money; to earn it, they work and drudge day and night; and when they have it, instead of using it to satisfy their wants and procure the comforts of life, or to do good with it amongst their fellow-men, they pile it up, and hide it, and watch it most carefully.

How much more prudent the followers of Jesus are in this respect! Their simple intention is to use the world only in as far as they have to do, and as God wills. Their hearts they keep free. While with their bodies they are on earth, they are soaring on high with God in the purity of their minds and the love of their hearts. Yes, the things they make use of in the world will be a help to them in raising themselves up to God. As mean and insignificant as a thing may be, look at it aright, examine it, study it—you will find it can teach you something about the goodness, mercy, justice, or power of God. Very appropriately, therefore, does Thomas à Kempis say: "There is no creature so little and so vile that it showeth not forth the goodness of God."

Let us do as Holy Scripture admonishes: "Love not the world, nor those things which are in the world. Mind the things that are above, not the things that are on the earth." We may use what we must of the world, as God desires it, for the honor and glory of God, for the welfare of our souls. This shall be our "simple intention." We will keep ourselves free from sin, mindful that we are ever walking in God's presence. This is the "purity of mind." How beautiful and true are these words of *The Following of Christ:* "As iron cast into the fire loses its rust, and becomes all bright with burning, so the man that turneth himself wholly to God is divested of all sloth and changed into a new man."

V.
Self-Consideration.

SOME of the ancient philosophers maintained that the foundation of all righteousness and morality lay in the following words; "Learn to know thyself." And they were not wrong. Why not?

God, in His infinite goodness and mercy, has revealed to us all we must know be saved. He has clearly told us what we must believe and what we must do in order to go to heaven. Jesus has also founded His Church to be our infallible guide on the way through this life to eternity. On the part of God, therefore, there is nothing wanting. He has pointed out the way clearly; He has given us an unerring guide; and He is with us to help us, by His graces, to overcome the obstacles that beset our path.

But on our part much may be wanting. We have mighty enemies to struggle with—the world and the devil; and they are very cunning and most treacherous; yet these enemies are only outside of the fort. The most dangerous of our enemies, the one that is the most treacherous, is the enemy inside of the fort—our own wicked natures. You understand this, don't you?

We are born with strong inclinations to evil; it is what we have inherited, through original sin, from Adam and Eve, our first parents. To do bad is natural for us, to do good goes against us. It is like going down and up a hill. Going down is easy enough; but climbing up is hard work. We are born with the root of one of the seven capital sins in our hearts. One has the root of pride in his heart; another, that of covetousness; another, that of lust, and so on. Some hearts, it seems, have the roots of all the seven capital sins fastened in them. Like Mary Magdalene, they are possessed by seven devils.

How very dangerous, therefore, we are to our own souls! We are liable, at any moment, to put out our hands, so to join by sin with the other two enemies, the world and the devil. We must ever be watchful over ourselves. We must study our natures, see what particular evil inclination, the root of what capital sin, we have fixed in our hearts. From time to time a sinful passion will show itself, or some bad habit may take hold of us. They spring up like the weeds in a garden, or the wild shoots round a tree. We must be on the watch, always; as soon as we see these wild shoots, we must cut them off, or tear them up.

Do you understand now what self-consideration is, and why it is so important to consider oneself? "If thou wouldst have true peace and perfect union," says Thomas à Kempis, "thou must cast all things else aside, and keep they eyes upon thyself alone."

A certain man inherited a rich, very beautiful vineyard. It was a very large vineyard, and in the best condition possible when he came into possession of it. All he had to do was to keep up his vineyard, work it aright, and tend it well, and he would become a rich man.

What did this man do? He was foolish indeed. He cared very little for his vineyard—very little he worked in it. He would rather attend to his neighbors' business than to his own. He would tell other people how to manage their farms, or how to work their gardens. He spent most of his time in idleness, or lounging around the public places of the town near which he lived. His own good vineyard he neglected nearly altogether.

What was the result? Let the Wise **Man** tell you : "I passed by the field of the slothful man," says He, "and by the vineyard of the foolish man, and behold! it was filled with nettles, and thorns had covered the face thereof; and the stone wall was broken down."

Apply this picture to yourself, my little follower of Jesus: If you care nothing about self-consideration; if you fail to examine yourself, to study your own faults, evil inclinations, and bad habits, your heart will soon be spoiled altogether, like a garden spoiled by the weeds, the thistles and thorns growing in it.

Do this in future: hold one eye fixed on God, to study and learn what is His holy will; the other eye keep fixed on yourself, to study yourself, to look out before you on the way you are going, that your foot may not be caught, that you may not stumble and fall. Do this; it will not leave you much time to watch others. You will have enough to do with yourself.

Let us finish with another passage from *The Following of Christ:* "The interior man regardeth the care of himself before all other cares; and he that looketh diligently to himself findeth it not difficult to be silent about others."

VI.

Joy of a Good Conscience.

MY little followers of Jesus, though you have everything else that you may desire, if you have not a good conscience you cannot feel really happy. You may have plenty of money; you may enjoy the best of health; you may be honored and esteemed by your fellow-men; you may have all the sensual pleasures you can wish for: if you have a bad conscience, if the secret worm of guilt is gnawing in your heart—this alone is enough to spoil all your joy and peace.

The sinner is blinded. He wilfully ties his own eyes, that he may not see the miserable, dangerous condition he is in. But as much as he may try to deceive himself, he will frequently feel the sting of his bad conscience, which fills him with alarm and uneasiness. Oh, if the sinner would only once look earnestly at himself, and examine the most pitiable, dangerous state in which he is on account of his sin, most certainly he would be frightened; and he would not tarry one moment to free himself from such a condition.

Here is a picture for us all to study; it represents to us the misery of those who live in the state of mortal sin.

A farmer in Italy was very expert in catching vipers. You know, the viper is a poisonous snake; its bite causes death in a very short time. The farmer would bring his vipers to the apothecary, who would buy them at a good price, for the purpose of making theriac, a certain kind of medicine.

One day the farmer had extraordinary success; he caught one hundred and fifty vipers; and he put them into a box which he always carried with him for that purpose. He was very tired when he got home. He took only a little supper, after which he lay down to rest. The box of vipers he set down on the floor, in one corner of the bed-room. What happened? While he was sleeping the vipers became restless: they began to move in the box and to press upwards. Thus it came that the lid of the box was forced open, and the reptiles crept out into the room. The warmth of the bed in which the farmer was sleeping attracted them. They, therefore, crept up into it, got in under the covers, and wound themselves around the man's legs and arms, and even around his body and neck.

Late next morning the farmer wakes up. Lucky for him that he awakes without making any motion. He forthwith realizes his condition, and he nearly dies with fright. Most horrifying, isn't it? The vipers encircling his arms, legs, and neck! One little motion, and they will be aroused; they will bite him, and the poison will be his death in less than an hour!

This is a picture of the sinner. Mortal sin, worse than a hundred vipers, has wound itself around the sinner's soul. Already the soul is dead; and it takes but a sign from God, in whose dread hand the poor, ungrateful sinner is, and the soul falls and is dragged into hell, there to be tortured forever. This the sinner knows, and he must believe it, and does believe it. How can he, therefore, be happy as long as he is in such a state?

Ah, yes! Like Adam, every sinner must say: "I heard Thy voice, and I was afraid." And with Jeremiah, the Prophet: "We looked for peace, and no good came: for a time of healing, and behold, fear." "Know thou, and see," thus admonishes the same prophet, Jeremiah, "that it is an evil and a bitter thing for thee, to have left the Lord thy God!"

Do you see now, my dear children, and understand why we should always strive to have a good conscience? "Have a good conscience," says *The Following of Christ*, "and thou shalt always have joy." Though everything and everybody should be against you in this world, have a good conscience, and you will live contented. If God is with you, if He is your friend, then you are all right. Serve God with a good conscience, and fear nothing else.

But I must finish the story of the farmer. What did he do to rid himself of the vipers?

For quite a while he lay immovable in his bed. At last he hears his son approaching the door of his room. He calls to him to be careful, and tells him, in a few words, what a terrible condition he is in. Then he orders him to bring a vessel of fresh warm milk and set it down in the middle of the floor.

This is done immediately. No sooner do the vipers smell the milk than they begin to untwist themselves from the man's limbs. They crawl down from the bed, and make for the vessel of milk on the floor. Now the farmer is free. He gets up from his bed quietly, takes the box which is standing in the corner, and puts it over the vipers around the milk. Thus the reptiles are caught once more, and secured.

First, he kneels down and humbly thanks God for having saved him from the death-bringing bite of the vipers. Then he managed, by the use of a pair of tongs, to draw the vipers, one by one, out of the vessel of milk, and killed them by cutting their heads off.

Let us not forget this : If we wish to live in peace and joy, let us keep a good conscience. If we have committed mortal sin, let us forthwith rid ourselves of the deadly viper twisting about our souls, by making a good confession. Cut off the viper's head by avoiding the old occasion of sin. Let us not fall back into sin again, and we may experience the truth of what Thomas à Kempis says: "Easily will he be content and at peace whose conscience is undefiled."

VII.

Love of Jesus Above All Things.

"IF any man love not our Lord Jesus Christ, let him be anathema," St. Paul writes to the Corinthians.

To say we love Jesus is one thing; to prove the love we profess for Jesus, by our lives, is quite another. It is easy enough to say: "O Jesus, I love Thee with my whole heart, and above all things." When there is something to be done, unpleasant and difficult for us, but pleasing to Jesus; or when there is something to be avoided, pleasant, perhaps, for us, and very tempting, but sinful, and therefore forbidden by Jesus—then is the time when we can show whether or not we love Jesus above all things; whether our love is only a love in words, or a love in deed and earnest.

Most of you, I presume, are acquainted with the history of St. Agnes, virgin and martyr of Rome. This saint, in her life and death, gives us such a beautiful example of true love of Jesus—I do not know what better I could do, by way of illustrating this chapter, than to tell you something of this great saint, her life and death. Listen, therefore, and take it to heart.

St. Agnes, when she was martyred, was only thirteen years of age. Her parents were rich, and of high standing in the city of Rome. Agnes was born a Catholic. She was a saint, even from her earliest childhood. As she grew up, and when she became older, she was filled more and more with a burning love for Jesus. She would love Him above all things ; He alone would be her Spouse ; she would not love another. Jesus was her All ; on Him she had her thoughts fixed constantly ; with Him she conversed in her heart ; in His presence she always walked, most carefully. You may imagine from this how modest, innocent, beautiful, really angel-like, this holy virgin must have been.

One day it happened that the prefect's son caught sight of her ; and forthwith he was captivated by her extraordinary beauty. His resolve was made immediately. He would woo her and make her his wife. His father, also, gave willing consent, and promised to support him in his suit for the hand of Agnes. And the saint ? She had chosen her Saviour, Jesus, for her Spouse ; would she now abandon Him to choose the heathen? Oh, no!

Her love for Jesus burst through all restraint; her words are like a burning fire. Listen to what she says: "Depart from me, thou food of death! Another Lover has come before thee, to whom I have given my heart and affection. To Him I will remain faithful; in His arms I trust myself, body and soul."

The prefect's son asks her who this lover is, and what kind of a man he is.

Again the Saint answers in terms of rapturous love: "My right hand and my neck He has adorned with precious stones; and to my ears He has fastened gems of inestimable value. He has clothed me with a mantle worked in gold, and beset with most precious ornaments. Honey and milk have I received from His lips, and His blood has crimsoned my cheeks. I am espoused to Him whom the angels serve, whose beauty sun and moon admire. My Spouse is Christ. With beautifying and sparkling gems did He adorn me. A mark He has set upon my face; I shall not admit any other lover but Him."

Thus did St. Agnes extol the spiritual gifts with which Jesus, her heavenly Spouse, had adorned her soul; but how could the matter-of-fact heathen understand such words? The holy virgin is now tied and dragged before the prefect's tribunal, to answer for her faith. True to Jesus, she refuses to adore the false gods, in spite of all the prefect's kind promises and flattering caresses. He commands her now to be led through the streets of Rome, exposed, for shame and disgrace, to the eyes of thousands and thousands of people; after which she is led into a house of lowest wickedness. But God watches over her; Jesus shields her innocence by several great, astonishing miracles.

Next she is put on a funeral pile, to be burned to death; but the fire does not touch her. The judge then orders the executioner to run his sword through her throat; as he trembles, St. Agnes cheers him up: "Why art thou afraid? Strike and kill this body, which is an object of pleasure for eyes which I do not want to please." The man now strikes and gives her the death-blow: and thus it was, my little followers of Jesus, that St. Agnes shed her blood and laid down her life in fidelity to Jesus, her Spouse, whom she loved most ardently and above all things.

Now, if you have *The Following of Christ* at

hand, or can get one, open it and read the seventh chapter of book the second; and tell me: Could you find anything better to exemplify this lesson about the "Love of Jesus above all things," than what I have told you about St. Agnes? Let us, therefore, ask Jesus to give us such a love. Ah, yes! we all feel it too well: our hearts are so cold! But Jesus says: "I am come to send fire on the earth, and what will I but that it be kindled?" Let us pray with the Psalmist: "I will love Thee, O Lord, my strength: in Thee I will put my trust."

"In life and in death keep thyself near to Jesus, and intrust thyself to His fidelity, who alone can help thee when all others fail!"— words from Thomas à Kempis.

VIII.
Familiar Friendship With Jesus.

OUR Lord most ardently desires our friendship; He will be our Friend, also, powerful and true; and He tells us what we must do to have Him always for our Friend. He says: " You are My friends if you do the things that I command you. I will not now call you servants: for the servant knoweth not what his lord doeth. But I have called you friends, because all things whatsoever I have heard from My Father, I have made known to you."

Do you see? Jesus has done everything to gain our friendship. Sin had made us enemies of His heavenly Father. To free us from sin, and thereby to reconcile us with His Father, the Son of God became man. The Child in the crib suffers and cries for the sins of mankind; the poor shepherds come, and the three holy kings, to offer Him their love and friendship. As a grown-up man, Jesus is reviled by the Pharisees, persecuted most bitterly by His enemies, in spite of all He does to draw them to Himself; the publicans, however—the "sinners," as the Pharisees called them—become the friends of Jesus. He eats with them, He converses with them, He stays with them in their houses. Mary Magdalene, the Samaritan woman at the well, are touched by His love and mercy for them; they repent of their sins; and forthwith He counts them among His friends. He calls Matthew away from the toll-house and makes him one of His apostles; He tells Zacheus to get down from the sycamore tree, because He wanted to abide that day in his house; and of the repentant publican in the temple He says: "This man went down to his house justified." Such, my dear children, were the friends of Jesus.

And when our blessed Redeemer was hanging on the Cross, suffering and dying, how was it? Even then His enemies hated Him; they scoffed at Him and did everything they could think of to increase His suffering. But even in that last bitter hour the love of the Sacred Heart of Jesus won a friend—the robber on his right side. Jesus said to him: "Amen, I say to thee, this day thou wilt be with Me in paradise."

And what now about the friendship of Jesus? Listen; Thomas à Kempis gives us the answer:

"Whosoever findeth Jesus," says he, "findeth a Treasure, yea, a Good above every good. And he that loseth Jesus loseth much, yea, more than the whole world.

A young man went over from America, across the ocean, to visit his parents, still living, and his brothers and sisters. He had not seen them for many years. What joy there was in that house! The old father and mother embraced their son and wept for very joy; the brothers and sisters, each in turn, embraced him—their dearest brother, for whom they had longed for so many years.

Two or three years after there came a parting. This same young man was drafted, and he had to go with his regiment. What sorrow and misery there was then in that house! The father was almost despairing, the mother's heart was torn. The brothers and sisters nearly went wild with grief. They all sobbed and cried aloud; they embraced him again and again; they clung to him as if they would force him to stay. But he had to go. Would he ever return again? Would they ever see him again, alive and well?

Such is life. A long-absent friend or relative returns, and people rejoice; he departs, and they are filled with grief. Let me ask: Is there a friend as good as Jesus? Is there a brother as loving as Jesus? When a soul finds Jesus, why do not men rejoice? When a soul loses Jesus by mortal sin, why do they not grieve and lament?

Let us, therefore, dear readers, always be friends of Jesus. It is not hard for us to gain His friendship. Was it hard for Mary Magdalene and the Samaritan woman to become friends of Jesus? They repented of their sins. So we, too, must repent if we have had the misfortune to commit a mortal sin.

On the Cross our Saviour could pray: "Father, forgive them, for they know not what they do." If we refuse the friendship of Jesus, He could not pray that way for us; for, surely, we know better who Jesus is.

If you are careful always to have Jesus for your friend, then it makes no difference whether or not you have other friends in this world. But, whatever other friends you may have, or whatever else you love, love no one and nothing more than Jesus. As *The Following of Christ* says: "Let all be loved for Jesus' sake, but Jesus for His own sake." If you have enemies, love them after the example that your Saviour Himself gave you. If you are thought well of and praised, think by yourself: whatever good there is in me, whatever good I am doing, all comes from Jesus!

Here is a sentence from *The Following of Christ*: " Without a friend thou canst not live happily; and if Jésus is not a friend to thee above all, thou wilt indeed be sad and desolate."

IX.

Want of All Consolation.

THOMAS A KEMPIS speaks from observation and according to general experience when he says: "I never found any one so religious and devout as not sometimes to experience a withdrawal of grace, or feel a diminution of fervor. No saint was ever so sublimely rapt and illuminated as not to be tempted sooner or later."

You must understand this aright. God never withdraws His grace from us in such a way that He will not assist us in time of temptation, so that, from want of this assistance, we must fall into sin. No! God is always with us; He always gives us grace enough to overcome the temptation. "God is faithful," says St. Paul. "He will not suffer you to be tempted above that which you are able; but will make also with temptation issue, so that you may be able to bear it."

By "withdrawal of grace" Thomas à Kempis means that God will sometimes take all consolation away from us. Outwardly we may be afflicted by various kinds of troubles, sickness, poverty, contempt from our neighbors, and so on; while inwardly we may be tried, at the same time, by most grievous temptations —temptations against charity, holy purity, and such like. Now, if in these trials and afflictions we could, so to speak, feel the loving hand of God supporting us; if we could lay our heads on Jesus' breast, as St. John did at the Last Supper; in short, if we could sensibly feel God's mighty presence holding us in His arms and sweetly consoling us: oh, yes! then we, too, might cry out in exultation: "If God be for us, who is against us? I am sure that neither death, nor life, nor angels, nor principalities, nor powers, nor things present, nor things to come, nor height, nor depth, nor any other creature, shall be able to separate us from the love of God, which is in Christ Jesus our Lord."

But, my little follower of Jesus, we must be tried even more than this. Jesus permits it. He Himself has deigned to give us an example of this. Look up to Him, as He hangs on the cross: His hands and feet are pierced by nails, thorns are driven into His head; His body is torn by countless wounds; His blood flows down to the earth; most intense is the suffering He endures—no one else, before or after, has ever endured such pain and torment; and all the while He hangs on the cross, He hears the bitter curses, blasphemies, mockeries from His enemies, those who have crucified Him, and for whom He dies. But the greatest pain, the most bitter of all torments He endures then when He cries out: "**My God, My God, why hast Thou forsaken Me?**"

So, let us be prepared for this want of all consolation, whenever and as often as God may visit us with it—prepared to take it with resignation, and endure it patiently, as long as it may last. It will be something in this way: you still have good will to say your prayers regularly, to make your meditations and examinations of conscience, to visit Jesus in the most holy Sacrament of the altar, to receive Him often in holy Communion, and so on. Heretofore you felt so much pleasure and satisfaction in these practices; but now, all at once, you lose your relish. You feel so dry and indifferent. When you pray it is nothing but distractions—no spirit, no pleasure. The same as regards your meditations and examination of conscience. When you go to church to visit Jesus, it is just as if He repulses you.

In Communion, though you continue to receive Jesus regularly and often, you feel as if it were not Jesus at all; He does not speak to you any more as He used to; He lets you be dry and without feeling, as it were. You become discouraged—you feel much like throwing everything overboard, that is, you are tempted to give up everything, praying, meditating, visiting the blessed Sacrament, receiving holy Communion, and all.

This is what is meant by "want of all consolation:" when the world, your friends, and, apparently, God Himself, have forsaken you and left you, as it were, to yourself. But courage! This is your best hour, my child! Hold on to your prayers and other practices, in spite of the dryness. You can gain the most precious merits now.

I read once about three pious sisters, who went together to church to receive holy Communion. Another saintly person was in the church and saw them. She had a vision in which she beheld our Lord, in the form of a Child, most lovely and gracious. When the first of the three sisters had received the sacred Host, Jesus very fondly embraced her, and, in look and manner, showed Himself friendly and loving. When the second received Him, He showed no more than ordinary satisfaction; He remained rather passive. But when the third received Him, our Lord showed nothing but signs of displeasure; He struggled in the priest's hands as if to get away from her; He put out His hands as if to push her away, and repel her. A voice asked —it was the voice Jesus Himself: "Which of these three, thinkest thou, gives Me most pleasure in receiving My Body and Blood?"

"Lord," answered the person, "most certainly the one who received You first."

"No," answered Jesus, "The one that received Me last gave Me most pleasure. The first receives Me only for the sake of consolation: I must draw her by sweetness, lest she come not at all. The second remains faithful, though she experiences little or no consolation from Me. The last, however, keeps on receiving Me, though I fill her heart with aridity and bitterness."

Do you see and understand?

I will close by giving you the example of David, as it is contained in *The Following of Christ:* "There was one who, when grace was with him, exclaimed: 'I said in my abundance, I shall not be moved forever.'

"But when grace was withdrawn, he tells what he experienced in himself, saying: 'Thou hast turned away Thy face from me, and I became troubled.'

"Yet even then he despaireth not, but more earnestly prayeth to the Lord, and saith: 'Unto Thee, O Lord, will I cry; and to my God will I make supplication.'

"At length he receiveth the fruit of his prayer, and witnesseth that he was heard, saying: 'The Lord hath heard, and had mercy on me; the Lord hath become my helper.'

"But in what way? 'Thou hast turned,' he saith, 'my mourning into joy, and Thou hast encompassed me with gladness.'"

X.
Gratitude for the Grace of God.

LET me translate for you a parable found in the writings of St. Ephrem. It is as follows:

"'He that hath, to him shall be given; but he that hath not, from him shall be taken away even that which he hath.' Is God unjust? No, indeed! Listen to a parable:

"A certain landlord had two servants and three yoke of oxen. To the one servant he gave two yoke of oxen; to the other, one; and he said to both: 'Go ye and work till I come back.'

"He that had received the two yoke of oxen went and worked with them diligently. By the good use of them he enriched himself; and lastly he fattened his oxen. The other, however, who had received only the one yoke, tied his oxen to the manger: sluggard that he was, he slept away his time without working in the least.

"After some time the landlord came back to see what his servants had been doing. He saw the work of the one servant, and the profits gained thereby, and he praised him greatly for it. He went also to the other servant: He found him sleeping; the oxen were still tied to the manger—so lean and weakened that they nearly fell over. He therefore said to himself: 'If I let this lazy servant keep my oxen I will quite lose them; he will let them starve to death. I know what I will do: I will take my oxen away from him and give them to the other, who has worked so well and cared so faithfully for his oxen; for to every one that hath shall be given, and he shall abound; but from him that hath not, that also which he seemeth to have shall be taken away.

"Thus, too, does our Lord speak to every one who is careless and neglectful: 'Because I am good, have I chosen thee, and given thee the faculty, by the performing of good works, to gain the possession of eternal life. But thou hast despised Me, and therefore will I also despise thee, and cover thee with confusion; because, wilfully, thou wouldst not agree to do good.'

"Now, is there injustice with God? Beware! Let us, therefore, dear brethren, endeavor most earnestly to make ourselves worthy of the love of God and of His saints."

So far go the words of St. Ephrem.

I spoke to you in the last chapter about the want of all consolation. The worldly-minded, lukewarm, careless Christian may not know and may never find out in reality what is meant by "the want of all consolation." How should he? He is only half and half. His maxim is: No more and no further than I just must, to. get to heaven Such a one our Lord does not draw into the sweetness of His intimacy. To follow Jesus from afar, so as not to lose Him altogether, satisfies him; to draw near and lay his head on Jesus' heart —nay! this is something he never thinks about.

But the true follower of Jesus, the faithful disciple whose continual and ever ardent striving goes to be ever near His Master; whose sole joy and happiness consists in being closely and intimately united with Jesus—he it is who sometimes, perhaps often, experiences what is meant by the want of all consolation.

Now, my little follower of Jesus, if ever that hour comes upon you, be it soon or be it later, then call to mind what I now write:

Go into yourself first and examine: **Am I the cause of this visitation?** Jesus has given you some particular grace, perhaps—not a great, wonderful one, with which to perform great wonderful deeds, but only a little grace, an enlightening of your mind, and a slight moving of your will to do some little good work. You have not been faithful; you have not taken the grace which Jesus offered you; you have not done the good work which Jesus wanted you to do. Did you commit a sin thereby? Perhaps not. But you were unfaithful to Jesus, nevertheless; and now He punishes you for it by withdrawing from you the sweetness of His consolation.

But suppose you are not at fault; you have not, knowingly, been unfaithful to Jesus, even in the least; what then? In that case, this withdrawal of consolation is only another trial of your love for Jesus, sent you by Jesus Himself. It is the best proof He could give you of His friendship and love. In either case, that is, whether this want of consolation is a punishment for you, or only another trial, take it with resignation, as I said before, and bear it patiently as long as it may last.

And now, here is where the gratitude for the grace of God comes in. Thomas à Kempis says: "This is the reason why the gifts of grace cannot flow in us, because we are ungrateful to the Giver, nor do we return all to the Fountain-head."

So it is. God has done so much for us, and He continues always to offer us new graces. But instead of thanking Him for the graces He offers us, we frequently disregard them, or even refuse to receive them. Therefore God withholds many a grace from us that He would otherwise bestow upon us for our further sanctification; and He gives it to others, more willing than we are, who receive it with gratitude, and make good use of it. Now, perhaps, you can find the meaning of St. Ephrem's parable; and perhaps you can tell why it is brought in connection with this chapter.

Yes, my dear children, let us ever be thankful to God for the graces He gives us. Whether the hand of Jesus strokes us consolingly, or whether it strikes us with tribulation, let us kiss it in humble gratitude; for, says *The Following of Christ*: "He that desireth to retain the grace of God, let him be thankful for grace when it is given, and patient when it is withdrawn. Let him pray that it may return; let him be cautious and humble, lest he lose it."

XI.
Lovers of the Cross.

ARE there many lovers of the Cross of Jesus? Thomas à Kempis tells us there are not. We study the life of Jesus, and we see it is all through a life of bitter, hard Cross-bearing. Not only did He carry the Cross on His way to Calvary—that was the heavy wooden Cross—but He carried it all the years of His life, from the first hour in the manger, to the last hour on Golgotha—the cross of poverty, hatred, and persecution from His enemies, the sins of the world, present, past, and future, the constant anticipation of all the sufferings He would have to undergo till the last day of His life. And what now about the followers of Jesus?

Our Lord speaks plainly enough: "If any man will come after Me, let him deny himself, and take up his Cross, and follow Me." Again He says: "The servant is not greater than his master. If they have persecuted Me, they will also persecute you." "Many are called,"—to be Cross-bearing followers of Jesus—"but few are chosen." "Enter ye at the narrow gate: for wide is the gate and broad the way that leadeth to destruction, and many there are that enter by it. How narrow is the gate and straight is the way which leadeth to life; and how few there are who find it!" Do you see now how it is?

However, you must not be frightened because of the Cross-bearing followers of Jesus there are so few. No, indeed! Go up to Jesus and ask Him to place His Cross on your shoulders: He will do so gladly; and He will help you carry it; and so you, also, will become a lover of the Cross, and you may count yourself one of the few.

You must not do like many: love Jesus only for the sake of consolation; go with Him, rejoicing, only till the breaking of bread; follow Him only as long as you see His miracles. You must love Him for His own sake; drink the chalice when He offers it to you; follow Him to the very pain and ignominy of the Cross.

A venerable hermit of the desert once entered the great city of Alexandria, in Egypt. He wanted to visit a sick friend, who had called for him to come and see him before he died.

Some of the people, seeing him enter the city, and knowing him by his garb to be a Christian hermit, gathered around him and began to laugh at him, and mock at his faith in Christ, and abuse him in every imaginable way. But he remained quiet, so meek and patient, as if they had not done him the least wrong.

Amongst other things, they asked him whether his Christ had also worked miracles. A stranger passing by, probably a Christian also, said to them, in answer to their question: "If Christ had not worked a single miracle, this should be miracle enough for you, when you see this holy man, from faith in his Redeemer, bearing so patiently all your abuse, so that, in spite of all your wanton insults, you cannot exasperate him."

See, my children, this hermit was a true follower of Jesus, an ardent lover of the Cross. So also must you strive to become. Be willing to give up everything for the love of your Saviour.

Though you may be "well fixed," as the expression is, that means, though you have plenty of money, so that you can get all the world can offer, be willing, for the love of

Jesus, and if Jesus so will it, to give up all your wealth, to live in poverty and lowliness, like Jesus. And if you have good parents, loving brothers and sisters, kind friends, be willing to lose them all for Jesus' sake; instead of these, be willing to have enemies and persecutors, like Jesus Himself; for He says:—

"Every one that hath left house, or brethren, or sisters, or father, or mother, or wife, or children, or lands, for My Name's sake, shall receive a hundredfold, and shall possess everlasting life."

You must be willing, moreover, to give up health, and all that you prize in connection with it, comeliness of person, your sight, your hearing, and so on—be willing to give up these for the love of Jesus, if so your Saviour should choose to visit you. But, how is all this to be understood? It is not said that you must really go and sacrifice all this—wealth, relations, friends, health, and so on. I said you must be willing to sacrifice these. You should be ready any time to make the sacrifice, if Jesus should desire it.

There is yet something else, better than those mentioned, which you must leave and give up for Jesus' sake. "What is that?"

asks *The Following of Christ.* "That, having left all things else, he leave also himself, and wholly go out of himself and retain nothing of self-love." That is, you must renounce yourself, your self-love, your self-will. Especially when obedience calls, then you must deny yourself. When your parents, or any other of your superiors, command you to do something, you must go forthwith and do it, however unpleasant it may be.

"If any man will come after Me, let him deny himself," says Jesus. "It is of less worth," says St. Gregory the Great, "to renounce what one has, but of great worth is it to renounce what one is." And Thomas à Kempis exclaims: "Oh, how much is the pure love of Jesus able to do when it is not mixed with any self-interest or self-love!"

This is to be a lover of the Cross.

XII.

The Royal Way Of The Cross.

WE have come now to the twelfth chapter of *The Following of Christ*—the last of the Second Book. It is a long, beautiful, very instructive, soul-inspiring chapter. If you have the book, or can get it, then read this chapter first, before you proceed with what I bring here for your special consideration. Read it slowly and carefully, every word and every passage of it—read it and meditate on it.

Now let us go on. We are told that to get to heaven there are two roads, on one of which we must walk: the road of innocence, or the road of penance. This is true. Either we must preserve our innocence as we receive it in baptism, that is, we must keep ourselves free from sin until death calls us away—and this is the way of innocence; or, if we have lost our baptismal innocence by sin committed, we must do penance, thereby to obtain forgiveness from God and atone for our sin—and this is what is called the road of penance.

But, considering it aright, we can reduce these two roads to one, namely, the royal way of the Cross, as Thomas à Kempis calls it. And how so? If you have sinned, if only venially, you must do penance, that is certain. What is that but going the way of the Cross? If you wish to preserve you innocence, to keep yourself free from sin, must you not fight with the enemies that pursue you, and struggle against and overcome their temptations? Must you not suffer persecutions from the world? For "all who will live piously in Jesus Christ, shall suffer persecution," says St. Paul. And what is this, again, but going the way of the Cross? Consequently, you see, the two roads merge into one—the royal way of the Cross; and for us, the children of men, there is no other road to heaven but this.

If, besides the way of the Cross, there were another road to heaven, most certainly our Saviour would have told us so. But Jesus teaches us by word and example that this way of the Cross is the only road to heaven. Be sure, therefore, if Jesus says of Himself: "Ought not Christ to have suffered these things, and so to enter into His glory?" be sure, I repeat, that neither you, nor I, nor anybody else will drive into heaven comfortably by means of a coach-and-four.

Very truthfully, indeed, does Thomas à Kempis say: "They who now love to hear and to follow the word of the Cross shall not then [on Judgment Day] fear the sentence of eternal condemnation."

Have you sinned? and do you intend, earnestly, to be a follower of Jesus? Well, then, prepare yourself for suffering. Jesus Himself will send you trials; they will come, sooner or later. If he does not send you any, or rather, if up to the present He has not sent you any, in spite of all your sins, then you ought to pray, and pray, and not give up until he sends you some. Why?

St. Ambrose, I think, it is, the great bishop of Milan, of whom the following is related: One day, on his journey, he came to an inn; and, as night was drawing near, he entered with his companions to lodge there till the next morning. He was there not very long when he began a conversation with the inn-keeper. He soon found out that the man was a wicked fellow, dishonest and an unbeliever. And he was rich; he had everything he could wish for, and everything arranged in the best manner.

The Saint asked him: "How are you getting along in your business?"

"Very well; I never lose, but am always gaining," answered the landlord.

"And you are always healthy, and there is no sickness in your family?"

"We never have to suffer from sickness," was the answer.

"You seem to have no trouble whatever of any other kind?"

"None whatever. Everything goes and comes as I wish it."

"Come, my brethren," said the holy bishop to his followers, "let us depart hence immediately. The curse of God is resting on this house; we must go away from it, lest the ruin that awaits it and its master fall on us also."

Only a short time after their departure from the inn they saw the walls of it tumble, and the roof fall in, and the godless inn-keeper, together with his family, was thus suddenly buried under its ruins.

Do you understand now? Let us, therefore, pray with St. Teresa: "Lord Jesus, let me suffer or die!" and with St. Magdalene of Pazzi: "Lord, not die, but suffer always!"

If you have not sinned—this is only s

posed,—for who is there that has the use of reason and has not sinned venially?—and want to preserve your innocence to the end, you must know and be convinced of it that you cannot do so (that is, with the assistance of God's grace) without undergoing a great deal of suffering and trouble. Therefore, one way or the other, you have no other road before you to heaven than the royal way of the cross.

Now, here are some points for you to take in and treasure in your heart for all your lifetime: First, in the Cross is your salvation; therefore, whenever and as often as Jesus lays it on your shoulder, take it and bear it patiently for His sake. Secondly, you cannot escape the Cross if you wish to be a true follower of Jesus. It is your only way to heaven. Thirdly, if you will not bear the Cross willingly, bear it you must; if you bear it unwillingly you can receive no reward for it. Fourthly, in bearing the Cross patiently for Jesus' sake, you will experience the only true joy that can be had on this earth; for Jesus assures us that "His yoke is sweet and His burden light;" and once the Cross will be your everlasting joy in heaven. Fifthly, whenever the Cross presses on you heavily, then think of your

Jesus carrying His Cross and dying on it, for you. That will give you new strength and courage to bear up.

For the conclusion, a word of admonition from *The Following of Christ:* "Take up, therefore, thy Cross and follow Jesus, and thou shalt go into life everlasting."

As it will take me more than another year to finish this work, I think it very good and useful to have this part of it—the First and Second Books—published, and sent on ahead. The Publisher has kindly offered to take the work in hand and get it out ; and, accordingly, it comes to you now in a cheap form. Instead of being left to lie idle, it is thus sent out, as much of it as there is, to work good in the world.—May it be a blessing wherever it goes ; and may God, through it, bless all those into whose hands it falls, and who read it !

In due time, God willing, the rest of this work will follow.

The Flowers.

"ONE summer evening, I was sitting out in my flower garden, in the shade of a large pear tree. It was sultry weather, and the air was rather heavy. I had worked hard all day, and was very tired. While my thoughts were wandering about among the days when I was a child, my eye-lids began to drop, and, after nodding a few times, I came near falling into a heavy sleep. But, all at once, I was aroused from the sleepy spell that was creeping over me by a tiny voice exclaiming, in words that could be quite easily understood: "No doubt, my friends, I am one of the most beautiful flowers in this garden. The Dahlia is renowned as such, far and wide. Who in the world doesn't know it? Just look at this rich bush of green leaves, from which I shine in the most exquisite red. Like a queen I tower on my bush, and can look down on you poor humble friends, creeping at my feet.

Where is the like to me?—Yes, I can say, I am about the only flower worth looking at."

"Don't be in too great a hurry, sister Dahlia, to put yourself at the head of all flowers," said the Rose; and you should have heard how snappish she was, when she said it. "You know, that honor belongs exclusively to the Rose. She is called 'the Queen of flowers,' and nobody else. You may boast of your fine red color, and the little else you can boast of—poor boasting, indeed! Why, the Rose can show you nearly every color under the sun,—red, white, yellow, pink, yes, even speckled the Rose can be! and, besides, such an excellent fragrance, as all the world knows! Where is your fragrance, sister Dahlia?"

"No rose without thorns," I heard the Tulip whisper, and I thought I saw her smile with as much affected grace as she could put on. "Who does not know, sister Rose, that you prize too highly your variety of color, and think too much of your fragrance? You shouldn't forget that you are full of thorns, so that the gardener can hardly pluck you without pricking his fingers. Methinks, you can't be very proud of your thorns."

"Sure, that's true enough! No Rose without thorns," added the Dahlia, and I could hear that she was very much vexed at the rebuke she had met with from the Rose.

"Look at me," continued the Tulip. "I am a flower that doesn't make much show at all. My stalk is quite plain and unpretending, as you may all behold; but what a rare calyx it bears. When the Sun rises in his glory, I open my cup to greet him, and when he sets, I give him another farewell-glance, before I close. Moreover, I have quite won the favor of our gardener, for being so fragrant. Not once does he pass, but he stops and refreshes himself by taking a full draught of my sweet odor. My friends, I am undoubtedly a beautiful flower."—

"Which we will not at all deny, sister Tulip," I now heard a Morning-glory say, that seemed to be quite earnest in climbing up the tall lath fence, near by. "Still, you are not the only flower that turns to smile at the Sun in the morning, and to sigh at his departure in the evening. I, too, have made that my fixed occupation, just as you did. Moreover, the Morning-glory (my name—the glory of the morning—is surely not without its signification; remember that, my friends!) is a flower of gaudy colors, mostly white, blue, or violet.

And how neat a cottage looks to have me climbing up its weather-beaten sides, adorning it with a coat of flowering green! Yes, I may say, without boasting, I am an ornament more fit for a house or garden than any other."

"You are an ugly braggart, sister Morning-glory," exclaimed a Poppy; and you should have heard how fretful the little thing was. "A great beauty, indeed! Why, people have so little regard for your beauty, they just trample on you."

The other flowers all giggled at this, and I saw how poor Morning-glory hung her head and blushed for shame.

"As for myself," continued the Poppy, in awful glee, "I am certainly a flower that is worth cultivating in a garden. First of all, you have the plant from which I grow, formed out of a most singular kind of leaves, the only ones of this growth in the garden. And then you behold the flower on the slender stem, like a full-blown rose, with leaflets red as carmine, and soft as the softest down. With all my compliments to your beauty, most graceful queen (and the Poppy bowed politely to the Rose,) I may say that I can almost vie with you in regard to beauty of color."

The fun, to see the Rose pout! She was just preparing to give a keen reply, when the Lily stopped her by bursting forth:

"Nonsense! Your beauty, sister Poppy, is the beauty of only one day. For a day you seem to shine and glory; then you fade away, and the next day sees you lying on the ground, pale and withering, as if you had been frightened to death by some hideous night-owl. You ought to be ashamed of yourself! Who would deem you worthy to be culled, and to shine in a bouquet? But the Lily is a flower before whom all the others may, in all humility, bow their heads; for, who must not admire her spotless white, and the excellence of her fragrance? My friends, do not forget, yes, never forget what our Redeemer Himself says of me: "Consider the lilies of the fields, how they grow:—I say to you, that not even Solomon in all his glory was arrayed as one of them" (Matt. vi. 29).

After these words of the Lily there followed an instant of hushed silence. Pretty soon, however, the other flowers all began to stir; and how they were piqued, at hearing the Lily's eloquent praise of her own beauty! They sat about, quarreling with her, each trying to lower her by extolling its own rare worth and exquisite qualities. While this noisy debate was going on, I caught a faint whisper, so faint, that it was not at all perceived by the rest of the flowers, and that I myself did, at first, not know from what quarter it came. I listened more intently, and behold! it was the voice of a Violet, hidden under the broad leaf of a Burdock. Most faintly it whispered, "Dear me, poor Violet! I am a mean, worthless flower, and though my Creator gave me a violet color and some fragrance to praise and glorify Him with, still, I am too ignoble to appear among the other flowers of the garden, which are all so sweet and beautiful. Let them give public praise to God; I will serve Him in private, as well as I can. To His honor and glory will I blossom here under this friendly burdock, and the little fragrance that I have shall be spent in humility, as an incense pleasing to His majesty."

Thus spoke the Violet; and this was the last flower I heard. For then I did, in reality, wake up. I had fallen asleep on my chair, and instead of being roused by the first words of the Dahlia, I continued to dream about the flowers. And in truth, there they were, the dahlia, the rose, the tulip, the morning-glory, the poppy and the lily, yes, even the violet under the broad burdock leaf,—there they were, all around me. Was it only a dream, or had they really spoken? I do not know. But I looked again at the violet; and I felt like preferring this poor, humble flower to all the rest —could any of you tell me why?

The Angels' Dialogue on New Year's Night.

GLORIOUS Christmas! How quick this happy day did pass! and now here's New Year just at the door. Everywhere so much joy and happiness at Christmas time —everywhere, except in Mr. Hamlin's house. Something there must have been that made things look so sad here. Josie alone, Mr. Hamlin's only son, a wanton boy of five years, quite full of boyish tricks, was just making the house ring all week with his merry shouts, and nothing could keep him back. Why? Because Christmas was just gone, and New Year was at hand, and naturally, he thought, all boys must be wild at Christmas and New Year. His baby sister, Emma, two years old, was a child of just the opposite disposition, quiet, and not noisy in the least. Her blue eyes, quite a world of angelic innocence and purity, looked very surprised at the frisks and shouts of her brother, as if she could not think what it was all about, since she beheld everything else so dreary. Well, she was only a baby yet; what do babies know about Christmas and New Year?

Where was Mr. Hamlin this last night of the old year? Not at home! He went to town pretty late in the evening,—no telling when he will come home, probably after midnight. He went to get his dram, as he said, "to warm himself up for the New Year." Well, he did the same on Christmas night, too, and he had done it for many a year,—gone to town at night "to warm up;" but no "warming up" for wife and children, for he never bought them a Christmas or a New Year's gift, nor did he ever think of going to the first Mass. How much did his poor wife long to go to this first midnight Mass, but no; he never let her go. She had to stay at home and watch the house, while he squandered many a week's earnings, purposely saved up for the Christmas and New Year's "spree." Well, he was in town again, this last old year's night, to get his dram for New Year.—Now you know what made his home so dreary! It's that way in all

homes where the father is given to drink;—
how sad!

His wife was waiting and waiting for him to
return; but he did not come. It grew late,
and she put Josie to bed, who was now sound-
ly asleep. Emma was lying in her cradle, and
her mother had to rock a long while, till she
went to sleep. The mother was rocking her
baby still, when her eyes, too, grew heavy:
her head began to nod, then it dropped, till
she was fast asleep on her chair. So they
were all asleep. And Mr. Hamlin?

The clock had just struck the midnight
hour, when he started on his way for home.
He had taken only one drink; then an inner
mysterious voice (his Guardian Angel's, perhaps) whispered to him: "Jim, that's enough!
Go home now; your wife is waiting for you."
He went. The dram-shop had no attraction for
him that night, he knew not why; and he felt
as he had never felt before. Something was
driving him home: "There you will be and
will make others happy!" He reached his
house, and from the distance he saw the light
through the window. On tiptoe he stepped
over the frozen ground, up to the window, to
take a peep at his loved ones, for he loved

them ardently, though he drank. What a sight! He saw them all three asleep. Josie in his bed, Emma in the cradle, and Hannah, his poor wife, drooping on the chair! More yet he saw:—God opened his eyes that moment, and he saw at the side of each of his sleeping children a tall, heavenly figure, each clothed in a robe of dazzling white, and bending over the children as if to guard and protect them. At this moment the Angels (for such they were—Guardian Angels) arose and turned to each other to speak. God, at this instant, opened the father's ears, also, as he had done just before with his eyes, and he could hear the Angels plainly, though the window was closed.

"Dear, innocent soul!" whispered Emma's Angel, looking fondly at the child. "There, that sweet smile! A dream is passing over the infant mind, and the smile is always a glimpse of a child's beautiful soul."

"Yes," said the other Angel, "if men had Angels' eyes, how differently they would look at a boy like my Josie."

"Indeed, it's so!" replied the first Angel, "men would then make less of the body, and care more for the soul. What is all the beauty of the body, if the soul is defiled? How it does shock my sight to look at a body with an ugly, sinful soul in it! And such a body is often considered by men to be an object of rare beauty!"

"Our God is infinitely good," remarked Josie's Guardian. "How horrid a body is without a soul in it! Men even shun it! God has no need of anybody; and yet He creates innumerable souls for the bodies of men to give them life. The soul is the breath of life for man, and is, so to say, the breath of God Himself, immortal, like its creator."

"And so my little Emma is a most precious work of God," added the Angel at the cradle. "If the child had only a body and no immortal soul, it would be no other than any other beast. But the soul in the body, being the breath of the holy God Himself, raises my darling, I think and dare say, far above any Angel in heaven. Why?—We Angels are only spirits; but man is body and spirit, and if he keeps his spirit holy and pure, his body will share the soul's future glory. Certainly, I am satisfied, and thank God, the Creator, that He has made and preserved me a pure spirit; but I pride myself on the commission I have, to protect and try to save such a precious creature as my Emma is. If I succeed in saving the soul, the body will be saved, also."

"A grand task, to save souls!" said the second Angel. "And I will do my best to save Josie, though the chances may be pretty well against me. If men would consider how precious a soul is, they would all strive to help us in our work of saving souls."

"Yes, indeed, they would, and parents first of all," added the other spirit. "When God created us, the invisible world, and then the things visible, He did so by a mere act of His all-powerful will. But when he was about to create man, He said: 'Let us make man to Our image and likeness,' as if He were going to do a hard or very important work. Well, God alone can create a soul, and it would seem He took great pains to create a beautiful one."

"In truth, our good Creator showed a great love for the immortal soul of man in creating it," thought Josie's Angel. "Though our glorious ranks were thinned by thousands, falling victims to endless perdition, God did not miss them; He was as rich and powerful as before; yet He determined to create man and give him a living soul, that he might, in course of time, fill out our vacant ranks. And He did so, though He foresaw that man would prove himself faithless, and countless souls would be lost. Still, the innumerable souls that would be saved were so lovely and precious in His sight, that He resolved to create man, though many might be lost, but only from their own fault."

"It makes me love the soul I have in charge more ardently, the more I think of it," said Emma's Guardian. "God did not only decide to fill up our ranks with the souls of men, but He even commissioned us spirits to aid Him in saving these souls. How dearly God must love a soul, that, after creating it, He will entrust it to an Angel's care, telling him to watch over this, His creature, day and night, never to abandon it, but to guard and protect it, as one would a costly treasure. How proud I feel of being instrumental in saving such a soul!"

"See what God has done furthermore for man's soul, dear companion," said the other Angel, "and we will surely never grow tired of our task.—Man was created. God looked down upon him infinitely delighted, as a father does on a child, and He thought to see the child of His hand ever happy in His presence. But no!

man turned away in disobedience and pride, and became an object of loathing in God's sight."

"So did our fellow angels, too," added the other heavenly spirit, "and the Creator, in His wrath, hurled them headlong into the bottomless abyss of hell. Didn't man deserve the same lot for his sin?"

"He did; and God, in His justice, might have punished him the same way," answered the first angel. "But remember, man's soul is the breath of God, it is His special property, and for this reason, I think, He did not want to punish man so dreadfully, because He loved his soul too dearly, and esteemed it, so to speak, as a part of Himself. How precious then, is a soul in the eyes of God!"

"Look there, the enemy skulking in the dark!" said Emma's angel pointing through the back window of the house. "He is prowling about after prey Let's have our eyes on him and watch him!—Precious, you say?" continued the spirit, picking up the former subject. "A real world God considers each soul to be, a world about the possession of which there is a mighty struggle between— whom?—Between God Himself and the devil.

'I will put enmities between thee and the woman, and thy seed and her seed,' said the Creator, when He promised to send His Son for the redemption of fallen mankind. Enmity between Satan and Almighty God! Enmity about what?—About man's soul!"

"Yes, man's soul was the object of Satan's envy and hatred from the very beginning," added the angel at Josie's bed. "Unfortunately he succeeded in getting this treasure into his power, and God took on Himself the great and hard work of tearing from the devil's grasp the victim of his hatred,—the soul of man. Hence the great struggle between God and hell, the object of which is man's precious, immortal soul."

"Four thousand years this great struggle was carried on," spoke the first angel, in turn, "and, sorry to say, Satan had the better almost all the time. How many souls he did capture all that time! At last God Himself, as He had promised, became man, to free the souls he loved so much from the bondage in which they were held by Satan. And a giant's work it was!"

"Well," remarked the other, "a God-man only could do such a giant work. What would we naturally say of a man, if we were to see him scourged, crowned with thorns, carrying a heavy cross to the place of his execution, and nailed to it hands and feet, a living man ? Seeing him hang on this gibbet for three long hours, a prey to the relentless fury of his enemies, the butt of all their most bitter gibes and revilings—what must we think?—This man must be a vile wretch, a great criminal, since his own fellow-beings treat him thus. But no, Jesus was nothing like this! And yet He suffered all this! What for?--To redeem His precious world, the soul of man!"

"Mankind was redeemed, when, by His death on the cross, the Saviour triumphed over the power of Satan. The enemy was weakened then, and heaven was again opened to receive those for whom Jesus died. Still," continued Emma's guardian, "the great struggle between God and hell is not over; it lasts as long as there is a soul to save."

"The enemy is as wily as before," added the other. "He is powerful still; and besides his numberless wiles and crafty tricks, he has two mighty confederates in this work of catching souls for hell—the world, and the corrupt, evil inclinations of man's own flesh.

What will become of my Josie?—Will he, one day, be a happy child of God, or will he be a reprobate slave of the devil!"

"Just as he wills," answered the spirit at the cradle. "That's all left to his own free will. True, the forces on the side of the enemy are powerful; but God fully does His part, too. If Josie, or my dear little Emma, will be lost, it's from their own fault. You know how much God has done and still does to save the souls of men. Besides redeeming them by His death, Jesus instituted a Church, replenished with His superabundant grace, which is to carry on the work of redemption in saving the souls redeemed by the death of her divine Spouse."

"Every child that is born has its angel to guard and defend it," said the Angel at the bed, lovingly spreading his hands over the sleeping boy, as if to ward off some hidden evil. "How lucky for a child if it is born within the fold of the true Church! The Guardian Angel will then gladly help invisibly to save the child; because, being visibly led by the hand of the true Church, the prospects are bright and consoling for the future."

"These two children have this great fortune," proceeded the other spirit. "They were cleansed by the waters of baptism. Being thus made children of the Church, they became children of God, and heirs of His heavenly kingdom. And, alas! the time may soon come when they will sin, and lose all, purity, grace, yes, God Himself and their home in heaven. The enemy is watching eagerly for this time to come."

"How ill men would fare," remarked Josie's Angel, "if Jesus had not instituted the Sacrament of Penance. After the first mortal sin that this child would commit, it would be hopelessly lost, had the Redeemer not opened a new fountain of grace for it to bathe and wash itself in,—the Sacrament of Penance. Another proof how dear and costly a soul is in the eyes of God!"

"In short, all the sacraments," rejoined the other, "what are they but so many strong weapons, given by Jesus into the hands of His children, through the ministry of mother Church?—The Holy Eucharist! If this alone does not speak out plainly how precious a soul is, then nothing does! Jesus, offering Himself up daily in millions of masses; then locking Himself up into the tabernacles, to abide there in solitude for days and years; and lastly, giving Himself over to men, by entering into their hearts, true God and true man, with body and blood, thus becoming the spiritual food of their souls, to strengthen them in the great struggle.—Oh, ye children, Jesus is making a continual sacrifice of Himself, to show you how highly he prizes your immortal souls, and to urge on you and all men the duty of doing all to save them," thus exclaimed the baby's Angel in a rapture.

"That's what God, the Holy Trinity, has done and still does, to save each single soul," said Josie's angel again, after a short pause of serious thought. "It makes me almost sad to see how many souls are lost in spite of all this, and just from their own fault,—souls that are so precious, and so beautifully ornamented through God's infinite bounty."

"Those three splendid gifts of the soul that make of it such a striking image of the Creator!" whispered the angel at the cradle, as if sunken in profound admiration. "Wasn't it by the Father's will that the universe was created, and isn't it by the same almighty will that all is governed and so beautifully kept in order in the whole world, above and below?—

As a type of His own omnipotent will, He puts into man's soul this first grand gift—the will."

"And what person of the Blessed Trinity," asked the other spirit in the same breath, "is, if we may say so, the universal *Memory* of God? Isn't it the Son, the future Judge of the word, in whose *Memory* all is present, no past, no future, but who will one day judge all ages and all men after His all-containing, never-failing *Memory?*—And the second gift in man's soul, the type of the Second Person in the Holy Trinity, and of the future, all-knowing, all-retaining Judge,—is the *Memory.*"

"How august is the *Intellect* of God!" continued Emma's Guardian in the same rapture of admiration. "In it is contained all the wisdom displayed by the Creator in building up the universe and making the laws that are to govern it; by the Redeemer, in the work of His redemption and the guidance of His Church for the salvation of mankind. The Holy Ghost, the Third Person in the Blessed Trinity, is the grand *Intellect* of God. He is called the spirit of wisdom and *Understanding.*—And now, the Third Person, too, wanted to be expressed in the soul of man by type, and hence He gave the third gift of *Understanding.*"

Therefore it is an angel's greatest pleasure," said the spirit, guarding the sleeping boy, besides contemplating God, the Fountain of all beauty, to be so near to guide and protect a soul, the soul being God's own living image, His miniature world, in which He loves to dwell. The Redeemer says: "If any one loves Me, he will keep My words; and My Father will love him, and We will come to him, and will make an abode with him." John xiv. 23). Even in the Old Law God affirms of Himself: "My delights are to be with the children of men" (Prov. viii. 31).

"What an overpowering thought!" remarked the Angel, looking at the baby in the cradle. "These souls, that are so very precious, whom God loves so tenderly, and for whom He has done, and daily does so much, —these souls are or were in the hands of parents, confided to their trust; and if God does all in His power, and though we poor angels work ever so hard,—it may all be in vain. In this great struggle between God and hell about a child's soul the child may be lost if it has parents that serve the devil, and, as his instruments, raise the child that God has given them to save."

"O my God!" sighed Josie's Guardian. "I would exult to see this boy die now, while he is young and sinless. For afterwards—Oh! my chances are poor!"

"The chances are poor for both of us, indeed," said the other angel in a sad tone. The mother is good, and tries her best; poor soul! But the father ——!"

"He will be the main cause, if these darling souls are lost," replied the angel at the bed. "The father is a drunkard; the son may become one, too. He is a wayward man, does not concern himself in the least about God and His holy religion; his son may follow his bad example. Then all our work will be useless, and the poor mother must deplore the loss of one or both of her children." "Indeed, mischief and sin seems to be born in the boy; for they frequently break out to view now, and will do more so the older he gets. The enemy knows, too, that prospects favor him; hence he is all the more on the watch to clutch these two innocent souls, as soon as the occasion presents itself."

"Perhaps he will succeed, alas!—said the Angel companion sadly. "Well, let us, at all events, do our utmost to save the little ones. Above all, we must unite our forces with those of the parents' angels, and then constantly work on the heart of the straying father. If we can bring him back to a better life, the prospect will be more favorable and we shall have reason to rejoice."

With these last words the vision disappeared. Mr. Hamlin could feel almost sensibly how the Angels of God, his own, that of his wife, and those of his two children, were making with united force an assault to capture and change his heart. Grace was working a miracle, because God knew that this was the hour when the poor sinful man would respond to His call.

For a few minutes the father stood immovable, as if stunned by what he had seen and heard. Never before had it been put before his eyes so clearly, how precious a soul is, as this New Year's night, when he saw the vision of the angels, and heard what they said. He then raised his right hand towards the starry heavens, as if he were about to make a solemn promise.—And he did promise: "O God, what a careless father I am! Thou hast given me four souls, that I must help to save—my own, that of a loving wife, and those of my two little children. Being a drunkard and a father unmindful of my holy religion, I have neglected to care for myself; and if I continue to do so, I may lose myself and those entrusted to my care—four precious souls! God of mercy! This night shall see me an altered man. Never more shall even a drop of liquor pass my lips, and as soon as the morning dawns I will go to make a good confession, and thus commence a better life, the life of a good Catholic, this first day of the new year. This is my promise: —help me, O God, with Thy all-powerful grace, that I may keep it and persevere."

After this he entered the house. His wife awoke, and imagine her surprise to see her husband come home with his senses sober, something he had not done for many a year. And how kind he was that night, asking her to forgive him for coming home so late, and promising that he would try hard, from now on, to make her happy. He stood awhile to gaze on his little ones; then he told his wife that they would retire to rest. He embraced her fondly, and her heart almost burst with joy; for she felt that God was working a change in the heart of her husband, though she knew not how and why.

The next morning, before Mr. Hamlin went to confession, he told Hannah, his wife, of the vision he had seen last night, and that he was resolved to amend his life, and become a good husband and father. He kept his word: and the consequence was, he felt happy, and saw about himself a family as happy as he could wish it. More than all—the prospect for eternity was brighter, too; for if parents, especially the father, take the lead by giving a good example, the children will naturally follow.

Would that this might move one or other wayward parent to return to God, before it is too late, and to make the family happy. "To day, when you hear My voice, harden not your hearts," says God.

Thus ends the story about the "Angels' Dialogue on New Year's Night."

The Legend of St. Christophorus.

I.

MY readers have often, probably, read stories about giants, so that it will be nothing new to them to read or hear one more. These giant stories are all very pleasant, as you will remember even from Bible History, when you read of the giant Goliath. What a braggart he was! "Am I a dog," said he to little David, "that thou comest to me with a staff? Come to me, and I will give thy flesh to the birds of the air, and to the beasts of the earth." Yes, indeed, the big-mouthed hero! The shepherd boy knocked him down with a stone and cut his head off.

Here comes another giant story; and though I would not warrant it to be as true in all particulars as that of David and Goliath, still, there is some truth in the story, anyway, namely: this giant did live in reality, and he is a saint in the Catholic Church, as we shall see farther on; whereas such heroes as "Jack the Giant Killer," together with all the giants he so bravely killed, are only imaginary persons.

Well, then, the giant! You all know who or what a giant is? He is a man much taller and stronger than other ordinary men. Just imagine that you see a man twelve or fifteen feet tall, twice as tall as a common sized man; think of his broad, heavy-set body, his huge head, his thick, strong legs, almost elephant like, his long, powerful arms and hands; in short, all in proportion to the height of his body, and you have a pretty fair idea of a giant.

Well, to begin with our story, there was such a giant once, many hundred years ago, and a mighty man he was, fully twelve feet high, strong and powerful. He was a heathen, and had a very heathenish name—Reprobus, the reprobate. This giant was very proud of himself, as naturally almost anybody would be, if he were such a giant. He had something of the nature of Goliath; he thought himself the strongest and mightiest man in the world, and that none could surpass him in deeds of strength and valor. He went about displaying his strength in all kinds of exploits.—Reprobus the giant!

But one day he took up a most curious notion. He thought by himself: I am the biggest and strongest man on earth. If I want to serve somebody, is it not becoming for me to hunt up the mightiest and most powerful king, and tender him my services? Why, certainly, the biggest man ought to serve the biggest king.—

> " The strongest man I am, a giant!
> No one like me, I hear them tell.
> Out I go to search the countries,
> Till a king doth suit me well.
> The mightiest lord of all the earth
> Shall have my service; only he,
> At whose name whole nations tremble—
> A giant king—the giant's lord alone shall be."

And out he went, Reprobus the giant, to wander through the world in search of the mightiest king. He walked about for a long time, and passed through many countries. Often he was told: "Here is the mightiest king," and again, "No there he is."—Just as it will be on the last day. "Lo, here is Christ," or "there He is."—But Reprobus was not so quick in believing all he heard; he went to examine, and he found that these were only petty lords, not at all worthy the service of such a famous giant.

At last he heard of one about whom all agreed that he was the mightiest king. Reprobus went to see. The king, he had to own, was a majestic man ; and everybody that came near him was over-awed. The king's palace was splendor itself, and the greatest pageantry round about the throne; innumerable almost were the officers and other persons belonging to the court. This monarch held powerful sway over many foreign nations, who would pay in their tribute most readily and with all marks of humble suppliance.

This was the man for Reprobus. He showed more power in his little finger than all the other petty kings did together ; and he concluded to enlist in his service. The king was glad to receive the giant among his court, and you may be sure he felt proud at having him in his service No one, he was certain, would dare to approach him with evil intent, as long as such a powerful giant was near to guard and protect him.

All went well. Reprobus was the king's most reliable servant, and felt highly pleased, yes, even proud, of being in the service of such a master, But—

"Once a minstrel, so goes the story,
  Entered the hall to play and sing,
And while a banquet the court was having,
  With harp and song he amused the king.
His ballads told of deeds of valor,
  And much he knew of Satan's might:
The king, on hearing the Devil mentioned,
  Blessed himself, which surely was right."

But not so thought the giant. In his blunt, straight-forward way he asked: "Lord king, what sign was that, and what did you mean by it?"

"It is the sign of the cross," replied the king. "If I make it, the Devil must flee and can't hurt me."

"The Devil? Who is the Devil?" again asked Reprobus.

"It is Satan, the Evil Spirit, the prince of darkness, who is always after. us, trying to hurt us," said the king.

"Then there is one still stronger than yourself, one that can hurt you?—King, I can't serve you any longer." I must seek him, whom you call Satan or Devil, and offer him my services."—

So spoke the heathen giant. The king tried in vain to retain him. He showed him how ridiculous and even how wicked it is to hunt up Satan for the purpose of serving him. But what did Reprobus know about the Devil? —He heard the king say that Satan had the power to injure him, the mightiest king on earth;—hence he must be a king more powerful than his present master; and having decided to serve the mightiest king, he determined to change masters. Forthwith he left the king's palace, and went out to hunt up the devil.

Dear readers, for the present we will let the giant go. Bad enough that he went out to serve the evil spirit! A little instruction, if taken, would have kept him back. But he was a heathen, and a giant full of pride.

A word, to parents: Every child born to the world, and reborn "of the water and the Holy Ghost," is a giant too,—not of the body, but of the soul.—Read again "The Angels' Dialogue on New Year's Night," and you will not forget how great, and, if we may say so, GIANT an object a child's soul is in the eyes of God.

Like Reprobus the giant, the little child wants to serve the mightiest king. The difference is: This heathen went out HIMSELF to hunt his master; he relied on his OWN SENSE of judgment to find out which is the mightiest king; whereas the child, with its precious soul, must BE LED to find God, to love Him, and to serve Him as the mightiest King,—and led principally by the parents! But if the parents themselves are not serving God, how can they lead their children to do so? Children will very often serve the very same master that their parents served. Christian parents, fathers and mothers, ask yourselves now: "Whom am I serving?"

II.

Reprobus, the giant, seeking Satan. Just think of that, children, how strange! And he hunted a long while. Not knowing what kind of a fellow the Devil is, he at first went along the public roads, the highways, thinking that, since these roads were traveled most, and, as he was told, Satan made it his task to trouble and hunt everybody, he would certainly find him there, if anywhere. But you know yourselves, children, the Devil doesn't come around in open daylight, so that everybody can see him. Or did he ever tempt you to do something wicked, when your parents or others might be around to watch you and catch you at the act? Sometimes, indeed, the Devil does "go about like a roaring lion, seeking whom he may devour;" but generally he avoids the highways, for fear of being seen and detected. He likes it best to prowl about in dark by-ways, and he gets plenty of victims there ; for those that want to sin leave the public highways, and go off into the dark. No wonder, therefore, that Reprobus could not find the Devil.

At last, being nearly wearied out, and almost despairing of ever finding Satan, he turned off and entered a by-road. And now it did not take long to find him.—

> "Behold, one night ('twas dark as pitch)
>   Twelve knights came riding on with speed,
> And in their midst, as black as Hell,
>   Sat one erect on fiery steed.
> A bunch of feathers, red as fire,
>   From his helmet waved in air,
> And his charger's hoof struck flames,
>   That lit the night and made it glare."

Boldly Reprobus stepped out into the road; and the wild troop came to a halt.—"Who are you?" asked the giant.

"I am the Prince of Darkness, and these are my companions."

"And whither are you going?"

"We are out on our nightly tour, making

booty, and taking prisoners for my kingdom."

" You look rather formidable ! "

" I am the mightiest king in the world."—(The Devil told a big lie here, didn't he children ? " WHO IS LIKE GOD ? " said St. Michael.)

" I am Reprobus, the famous giant."

" I know it."

" You are the Prince of Darkness, also called Satan or Devil ? "

" Just as you say."

" Will you accept my services ? I've been seeking you for a long while."

" I know you have, but not on the right road.—I came this way to-night on purpose to meet with you. You are welcome to my service, and I shall be proud to number such a famous giant among my followers. Get a horse to suit yourself and follow me. You will find me a kind and indulgent master—(yes, indeed !) and a mighty lord. I will rely on your giant strength and, accordingly, I expect giant deeds of war and fighting. Work bravely;—I will in time give you due reward."—(Good God ! what a reward would the giant get ?)

Reprobus soon had a horse, and a powerful fellow he was, just the horse he wanted. And thus he joined Satan's band.

A wild life he now led, roaming about all over the country, to the terror of everybody. Satan was highly pleased and prided himself ever so much on his precious acquisition,—the powerful, heathen giant. Reprobus soon found how mighty a king, indeed, Satan is; and the wild life in his new master's service was just what a giant like himself desired. But, thank God, things soon took another turn.

> "One night, while on their hidden ways
>   The Prince of Hell his band was leading,
> They met a cross quite unawares,
>   With Jesus crucified and bleeding.
> As soon as Satan saw the cross,
>   In trembling fear he took to flight,
> And after him, with cries of terror,
>   His followers all fled through the night."

Reprobus fled, too, though he knew not why. He had to spur his steed till the beast almost grew furious, and in spite of this could hardly keep up with his fleeing master. At last, coming up with him, he demanded: "Master, what does this sudden turn and hurrying off signify?"

"The cross!" gasped the Devil.

"That sign by the wayside? What of that?—It is only a piece of wood."

"Only a piece of wood! Don't you know who is hanging on that piece of wood?"

"Some wicked criminal, I presume, dying for his crimes."

"No, indeed!" answered Satan in the utmost fury. "It is Jesus Christ. I instigated men to nail Him to the cross; but, woe to me! when He died He broke my power, and ever since I have to flee before the cross."

"Who is this Jesus Christ?—and how could He break your power when He died?"

"He is true God and true man, my Lord and Master. After His death, He rose again to life. Against Him goes all my warring, but, oh! I am weakened in power."

Thus spoke the Devil with a hollow voice. (Who forced this confession from him?)

"One mightier than you?" asked the giant, surprised at the unexpected confession. "Lord Satan, I can't stay with you any longer. I must hunt up Him whom you call Jesus Christ, true God and true man; He shall be my Lord and Master; Him will I serve."— And without another word the giant turned and left the Devil's service.

"Another servant gone!" and the Devil

gnashed his teeth in fury. "Cursed be the Nazarean for this work!"

Let us stop here again, just a little. Dear readers, large and small, you have heard how proud the Devil felt of having such a giant in his service. A giant can do a giant's work.

Satan, in our days, is out hunting his prey— precious, immortal souls—with as untiring a zeal as. ever. He lost heaven, and out of hatred to God he wants to keep as many of us as possible from taking his place.—Who can doubt that many children, even when quite small, are entrapped by Satan, because of their parents lacking in watchfulness? Is this only a dream, or a trite saying, because so often repeated?—Would to God, it were so! I have just before me a book treating on "The Most Important for Parents, Teachers, and Guardians of Youth, consequently also for Pastors." I wish I could place this book in the hands of every parent, and then, when they have all read it, let one say that it is not important.

If parents are not thoroughly religious, sound, earnest-minded Catholics; if they have no control over their passions, but give them free vent, just as they desire it, and thus serve sin in many ways, what will become of the little ones? They are born with an inclination to the sins of their parents; these sins, daily committed, will make deep impressions on their youthful hearts. Parents being given to such ways are naturally careless and will not watch; they will not see the dangers to which their children are exposed; and hence they will not warn, correct, or punish them, when it ought to be done:—and what follows from all this? Many children get into the fangs of Satan, even when very young, by means of their own parents, and afterwards will be powerful instruments in misleading others. Being giants in sin, they do a giant's work in the Devil's service.—Hence, dear father and mother, the question so important for you to ask and answer: "Whom am I serving?"

III.

Reprobus wandered about for a long time, searching for the mighty King called Jesus Christ, the Crucified; but since the whole world nearly was still pagan, sunk in idolatry, nobody could tell him where to find Jesus Christ.

One evening, much wearied by the day's journey, he came to a thin, lonely woods, and in it he found a hut, with an old, venerable-looking man (one of the early hermits, I suppose) living in it. He asked the hermit to let him pass the night near his hut in the woods, for he was very tired from walking so far.

The hermit, at first surprised, almost frightened, at seeing before him such a giant, strong enough to carry his little hut with himself in it away on his shoulders, asked him where he came from, whither he was going, and what was his occupation.

"I am seeking a King called Jesus Christ," answered the giant, "and though I learned for sure that He is the mightiest King, I can't find Him, nobody knows where He is."

The hermit looked surprised, then a smile lit his venerable face. "Thank this mighty King you are seeking, my friend," said he, "for He has guided you at last to a place where you can be taught to know, love, and serve Him."

"Do you, then, know the King called Jesus Christ?" asked Reprobus quickly.

"In truth, I do, and can tell you all about Him."

"Is it the one called the Crucified?"

"It is.—He died on the cross for us."

"Did He overcome a certain king called Prince of Darkness, Satan, or Devil, when He died on the cross?"

"He did. By His death, He freed us all from the bondage of this wicked tyrant.—On the cross He broke Satan's power."

"Just as I heard!" exclaimed the giant. "And is this Jesus, the Crucified, living?"

"Yes. After three days He rose from the grave, in sign of His victory."

"Oh, then tell me all about Jesus Christ, where I can find Him, and how I must serve Him."

The hermit first asked Reprobus to explain how he came to hear of Jesus Christ, the Crucified; and the giant narrated to him all the adventures he had passed through while searching for the mightiest king.

"Had you been wise and more humble," remarked the hermit, after having heard the giant's story, "you might have found Jesus Christ before this. Didn't the first king you were serving make the sign of the cross, as he said, in order that Satan might not hurt him? Had you asked more about that sign than about Satan, you would even then have learned all about Jesus Christ. Now, my friend, let me in a few words tell you about this 'mightiest King,'—Who He is, what He did for us, and how you must serve Him."

The hermit began. He told him about God—the One God in Three Divine Persons; how God created the angels, and how they fell; how, then, man was made, to take the place of the fallen angels; how he sinned, however, and lost Paradise; how God promised a Redeemer and that after four thousand years this long-expected Redeemer came. Reprobus next learned who was the Mother of Jesus, and where He was born; how He lived, and all that happened to Him during His life; how much good He did, for which His own people nailed Him to the cross; that, however, after three days, He rose again from the dead, and, after establishing His Church, ascended into heaven, whence He would one day come again to judge the world.

The saintly old man told him all at full length, just as children are taught in their catechisms; for though Reprobus was a giant of body, he was a child as to religion, and the instruction lasted for several hours.

With profound reverence he listened to the words flowing from the hermit's lips. "How great and powerful is this God!" said the giant. "How merciful towards us poor unworthy creatures, to send His only Son to save us! Now I see why the hatred of Satan is so great, and why he flees before the cross."—

> "Yes, mighty is the Lord our God,
>   The world proclaimed His sovereign power.
> From pole to pole He governs all,
>   Most distant star, the lowest flower.
> And God, in His decrees of mercy,
>   Hath sent to us His only Son,
> Who from the devil's bondage freed us,
>   And back for God His creatures won.
> We may again call God our Father,
>   And Jesus is our loving Friend.
> If here we truly love Him, serve Him,
>   He gives us heaven in the end."—

Thus sang the hermit in holy rapture.

"What must I do to serve Jesus the Crucified?" asked Reprobus.

"You must follow the example of this same Jesus, your Master," replied the hermit. "You must lead a life of mortification. You must pray, watch, and fast."

"Pray, watch, and fast! What is that?"

The hermit explained in a few words,—and

right off the giant's countenance fell.—" If you know of no better way for me to serve this mightiest of kings, venerable sir, then I must give up the idea of serving him altogether. I know nothing about praying; I must have my full sleep; and a man like myself cannot fast."

"Well, my friend," said the hermit, "I do know of a better way for you to serve your Master, one more suited to a giant. Not far from here there is a pretty large stream, over which there is no bridge. Just now there is also no one to carry the wanderers over, when they want to cross from bank to bank. This is the work for you. Go you, and build a hut on the bank of the stream, and in all humility, out of love to Jesus crucified, carry every one across that calls upon you."—With this Reprobus was satisfied, and thus both retired for the night.

The next morning they built a suitable habitation on one of the banks of the river, and after having appointed a certain time of the day for his disciple to come over for further instructions, the hermit returned to his own little hut.

Reprobus was well pleased with his new employment. Daily he learned more about the great God he was serving, and the oftener he conversed with his teacher, the stronger grew his love for Jesus, his Saviour.

One dark, stormy night the giant was sitting in his spacious hut, listening to the wind as it was howling over the river banks, and in the woods near by. All at once he thought he heard a child's voice outside. No, it was only the storm moaning about his hut. But now he hears the voice again. Up he starts and steps out, and there, on the bank, he sees a child, a little boy of not more than four years, waiting to be carried across. "Please, sir, take me across the river."

"Why, my child, what can you want across the river such a night as this? Where are you from, and how did you get here?"

"Don't ask," said the child kindly, "but take me over."

Reprobus, mindful of the words of his instructor, "never to ask, but willingly to take each wanderer over," got his staff (the rough, torn-off branch of a tree, by the way), and softly taking the child on his shoulders, he fearlessly stepped into the stream.

When he came near the middle of the river,

he perceived that the water was rising on him—it was coming higher and higher. At the same time the child on his shoulders was getting heavier. Large drops of sweat stood on his brow, he grew unsteady, and feared to lose his footing.

"O, child!" he at last broke forth; "what a weight you are for me! It is as though the whole world were resting on my shoulders."

"Not only the whole world," answered the child's sweet voice; "thou art carrying Him who made the world. And that thou mayest know that I am Jesus Christ, thy Lord and Master"—so saying the Child dipped the giant under water, and baptized him, calling him Christophorus, "Christ-carrier"—"that you may believe, and be true to Me," continued the Child, "when you leave the river, stick your staff into the ground; tomorrow you will find it green and full of blossoms." With these words the Child disappeared. Reprobus, now Christophorus, did as the Child Jesus had told him: he stuck his staff into the ground on the bank of the river, and the next morning it had leaves and blossoms.

The rest of the giant's story is short. Christophorus continued in his employment at the river for a long while; and the hermit was, as yet, his best friend, his guide in the service of God. The giant was faithful to the end. Being taken prisoner by a horde of wild men, he was led before their king, and refusing to renounce Christ and His holy religion, he was put to death. We, therefore, venerate him as a glorious martyr of God—St. Christophorus—each year, on the 25th of July.

Dear readers, when does the giant appear to you to be the greatest? He was the proud vassal of an earthly king; he then became the dread follower of Satan; but lastly he humbled his pride, and became the faithful servant of Christ. Humility obtained for him the singular favor of being permitted to carry the Child Jesus on his shoulders.

"Whosoever, therefore, shall humble himself as a little child, he is the greatest in the kingdom of heaven" (Matt. xviii. 4).

THE END.

PUBLICATIONS

OF

P. J. KENEDY,

Excelsior Catholic Publishing House,

5 BARCLAY ST., NEAR BROADWAY, NEW YORK,

Opposite the Astor House

Adventures of Michael Dwyer...	$1 00
Adelmar the Templar. A Tale...	40
Ballads, Poems, and Songs of William Collins...	1 00
Blanche. A Tale from the French...	40
Battle of Ventry Harbor...	20
Bibles, from $2 50 to...	15 00
Brooks and Hughes Controversy...	75
Butler's Feasts and Fasts...	1 25
Blind Agnese. A Tale...	50
Butler's Catechism...	8
" " with Mass Prayers...	30
Bible History. Challoner...	50
Christian Virtues. By St. Liguori...	1 00
Christian's Rule of Life. By St. Liguori...	30
Christmas Night's Entertainments...	60
Conversion of Ratisbonne...	50
Clifton Tracts. 4 vols...	3 00
Catholic Offering. By Bishop Walsh...	1 50
Christian Perfection. Rodriguez. 3 vols. *Only complete edition*...	4 00
Catholic Church in the United States. By J. G. Shea. Illustrated...	2 00
Catholic Missions among the Indians...	2 50
Chateau Lescure. A Tale...	50
Conscience; or, May Brooke. A Tale...	1 00
Catholic Hymn-Book...	15
Christian Brothers' 1st Book...	13

Catholic Prayer-Books, 25c., 50c., up to 12 00

☞ Any of above books sent free by mail on receipt of price. Agents wanted everywhere to sell above books, to whom liberal terms will be given. Address

P. J. KENEDY, Excelsior Catholic Publishing House, *5 Barclay Street, New York.*

Christian Brothers' 2d Book	$0 25
" " 3d "	63
" " 4th "	88
Catholic Primer	6
Catholic School-Book	25
Cannon's Practical Speller	25
Carpenter's Speller	25
Dick Massey. An Irish Story	1 00
Doctrine of Miracles Explained	1 00
Doctrinal Catechism	50
Douay "	25
Diploma of Children of Mary	20
Erin go Bragh. (Sentimental Songster.)	25
El Nuevo Testamento. (Spanish.)	1 50
Elevation of the Soul to God	75
Epistles and Gospels, (Goffine.)	2 00
Eucharistica; or, Holy Eucharist	1 00
End of Controversy. (Milner.)	75
El Nuevo Catecismo. (Spanish.)	15
El Catecismo de la Doctrina Christiana. (Spanish Catechism)	15
El Catecismo Ripalda. (Spanish)	12
Furniss' Tracts for Spiritual Reading	1 00
Faugh a Ballagh Comic Songster	25
Fifty Reasons	25
Following of Christ	50
Fashion. A Tale. 85 Illustrations	50
Faith and Fancy. Poems. Savage	75
Glories of Mary. (St. Liguori.)	1 25
Golden Book of Confraternities	50
Grounds of Catholic Doctrine	25
Grace's Outlines of History	50
Holy Eucharist	1 00
Hours before the Altar. Red edges	50
History of Ireland. Moore. 2 vols	5 00
" " O'Mahoney's Keating	4 00
Hay on Miracles	1 00
Hamiltons. A Tale	50
History of Modern Europe. Shea	1 25
Hours with the Sacred Heart	50
Irish National Songster	1 00
Imitation of Christ	40
Catholic Prayer-Books, 25c., 50c., up to	12 00

☞ Any of above books sent free by mail on receipt of price. Agents wanted everywhere to sell above books, to whom liberal terms will be given. Address

P. J. KENEDY, Excelsior Catholic Publishing House,
5 Barclay Street, New York.

Irish Fireside Stories, Tales, and Legends.
(Magnificent new book just out.) About 400 pages large 12mo, containing about 40 humorous and pathetic sketches. 12 fine full-page Illustrations. Sold only by subscription. Only **$1 00**
Keeper of the Lazaretto. A Tale **40**
Kirwan Unmasked. By Archbishop Hughes **12**
King's Daughters. An Allegory **75**
Life and Legends of St. Patrick **1 00**
Life of St. Mary of Egypt **60**
" " *Winefride* **60**
" " *Louis* **40**
" " *Alphonsus M. Liguori* **75**
" " *Ignatius Loyola.* 2 vols **3 00**
Life of Blessed Virgin **75**
Life of Madame de la Peltrie **50**
Lily of Israel. 22 Engravings **75**
Life Stories of Dying Penitents **75**
Love of Mary **50**
Love of Christ **50**
Life of Pope Pius IX **1 00**
Lenten Manual **50**
Lizzie Maitland. A Tale **75**
Little Frank. A Tale **50**
Little Catholic Hymn-Book **10**
Lyra Catholica (large Hymn-Book) **75**
Mission and Duties of Young Women **60**
Maltese Cross. A Tale **40**
Manual of Children of Mary **50**
Mater Admirabilis **1 50**
Mysteries of the Incarnation. (St. Liguori.) ... **75**
Month of November **40**
Month of Sacred Heart of Jesus **50**
" " *Mary* **50**
Manual of Controversy **75**
Michael Dwyer. An Irish Story of 1798 .... **1 00**
Milner's End of Controversy **75**
May Brooke; or, Conscience. A Tale **1 00**
New Testament **50**
Oramaika. An Indian Story **75**
Old Andrew the Weaver **50**
Preparation for Death. St. Liguori **75**

Catholic Prayer-Books, 25c., 50c., up to 12 00
☞ Any of above books sent free by mail on receipt of price. Agents wanted everywhere to sell above books, to whom liberal terms will be given. Address

P. J. KENEDY, Excelsior Catholic Publishing House,
5 Barclay Street, New York.

Prayer. By St. Liguori.	$0 50
Papist Misrepresented	25
Poor Man's Catechism	75
Rosary Book. 15 Illustrations	10
Rome: Its Churches, Charities, and Schools. By Rev. Wm. H. Neligan, LL.D.	1 00
Rodriguez's Christian Perfection. 3 vols. Only complete edition	4 00
Rule of Life. St. Liguori	40
Sure Way; or, Father and Son	25
Scapular Book	10
Spirit of St. Liguori	75
Stations of the Cross. 14 Illustrations	10
Spiritual Maxims. (St. Vincent de Paul)	40
Saintly Characters. By Rev. Wm. H. Neligan, LL.D.	1 00
Seraphic Staff	25
" *Manual,* 75 cts. to	3 00
Sermons of Father Burke, plain	2 00
" " " gilt edges	3 00
Schmid's Exquisite Tales. 6 vols	3 00
Shipwreck. A Tale	50
Savage's Poems	2 00
Sybil: A Drama. By John Savage	75
Treatise on Sixteen Names of Ireland. By Rev. J. O'Leary, D.D.	50
Two Cottages. By Lady Fullerton	50
Think Well On't. Large type	40
Thornberry Abbey. A Tale	50
Three Eleanors. A Tale	75
Trip to France. Rev. J. Donelan	1 00
Three Kings of Cologne	30
Universal Reader	50
Vision of Old Andrew the Weaver	50
Visits to the Blessed Sacrament	40
Willy Reilly. Paper cover	50
Way of the Cross. 14 Illustrations	5
Western Missions and Missionaries	2 00
Walker's Dictionary	75
Young Captives. A Tale	50
Youth's Director	50
Young Crusaders. A Tale	50
Catholic Prayer-Books, 25c., 50c., up to	12 00

☞ Any of above books sent free by mail on receipt of price. Agents wanted everywhere to sell above books, to whom liberal terms will be given. Address

P. J. KENEDY, Excelsior Catholic Publishing House,
5 Barclay Street, New York.

www.ingramcontent.com/pod-product-compliance
Lightning Source LLC
Chambersburg PA
CBHW021346230426
43666CB00006B/423